John Lucas is the author of four books,
London's 100 museums. He was born in
London, and can trace his family back to
Benington, in Hertfordshire, in 1750. He now lives in Potters Bar and
has spent more than a year gathering information about the curiosities
included in the book, visiting and photographing all of them. He began
in journalism as a reporter on the Barnet Press, later becoming a
founder member of *The Sunday Telegraph*. He is now on the staff of *The
Daily Telegraph*.

Frontispiece
The figure of Venus found near the Verulamium
Roman theatre at St Albans

Hertfordshire Curiosities

John Lucas

THE DOVECOTE PRESS

First published in 1990 by The Dovecote Press Ltd
Stanbridge, Wimborne, Dorset BH21 4JD

ISBN 0 946159 75 0

© John Lucas 1990

Reprinted 1992, 1993

Phototypeset in Times by The Typesetting Bureau
Wimborne, Dorset
Printed and bound in Singapore

Contents

Introduction

The narrow, twisting lanes of rural Hertfordshire are woven into the tapestry of my childhood memories – a half-remembered dream, but now often refreshingly recaptured since I have made my home there. Even today, the county remains largely green and peaceful, and E. M. Forster's comment that 'Hertfordshire is England meditative', remains true.

But this book is about another aspect of the county's personality – its 'curious' side. 'Curiosity' is admittedly a subjective term, for what seems curious to me may not appear so to others. To me a curiosity is something strange, fascinating, unexpected, or at least interesting – or perhaps an amalgam of some or all of these – and I hope these characteristics are amply represented here.

Certainly Hertfordshire has proved to be full of surprises. It could be a monument to a slave-trade reformer that you may pass every day without realising it is there; the stamping ground of a notorious woman highwayman; a famous war leader's burial place; Black Death graffiti; the working desk of a great playwright, or houses where a king's assassination was planned and the Gunpowder Plot foiled.

In noting places of interest, I have also tried not only to sketch in people or events, but to fit them into their historical context.

I can only hope you enjoy your explorations into little-known Hertfordshire as much as I have done.

John Lucas

NB: Peaceful the county may be, but not, alas, vandal-free. Some of the items described are in village churches, which have to be locked more often than they were. The best opportunity for visiting them is, of course, around the time of services.

Acknowledgements

For help during the compilation of this book I should like to thank the following: Janet Pleshette for her companionship and encouragement; Jean Gardner for the benefit of her researches on Flowton Priory and Hertfordshire puddingstone; Malcolm Lang, for help with picture production; Mary Rensten, for permission to reproduce her brass-rubbing of the Hunsdon park-keeper brass; my son Jonathan for his sketch of Ye Olde Fighting Cocks, St Albans; also Judy Almond, Hugh Baddeley, George Cobham, Robert Dimsdale, Peggy Dunckley, John Farnham, Henry W. Gray, John Huntley, Les and Liz Kitto, Robert Pearson, Dudley Plummer, Dr Violet Rowe, Barbara Taylor and Janet Watson.

I am also grateful to helpful staff of Hatfield House, Knebworth House and Brocket Hall, and to the excellent Local Studies Centre library at County Hall, Hertford, and the librarians of town libraries and museums for source material and guidance; and the many members of the clergy and laity of county churches for information and interest.

For permission to take photographs, I thank the National Trust in respect of Shaw's Corner, Ayot St Lawrence (custodian, Mrs Diane S. Uttley), The First Garden City Heritage Museum, Letchworth (curator, Robert Lancaster), and the trustees of the Rhodes Memorial Museum (curator, David Parry).

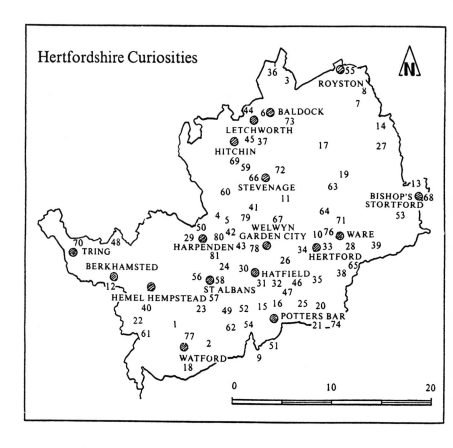

Hertfordshire Curiosities

1 Birthplace of England's Only Pope

Position: Abbots Langley, south-east of Hemel Hempstead.
O.S. Map: Luton & Hertford area; Sheet 166; 1/50,000.
Map Ref: TL 095/023.
Access: St Lawrence's church is off the High Street.

The tablet on the south wall inside St Lawrence's Church notes the
parish as the birthplace of England's first and only Pope: Nicholas
Breakspear, who became Adrian IV in Henry II's time, from 1154 to
1159. He is said to have been born in around 1100 somewhere in the
hamlet of Bedmond, a mile or so north of the church, across the M25.
Another possible place is on the site of the present 17th-century farm of
Breakspears, where Breakspear Way joins the M1 (junction 8) on the
eastern edge of Hemel Hempstead, about two miles north of Bedmond.

   Breakspear's story is a strange one. His father, a poor man, became a
monk at St Albans Abbey, but Nicholas was thought to be too young
and too ignorant, so his application to follow his father was rejected.
Disappointed, he eventually went to France and became a canon in
Provence, then – on account of his intelligence! – an abbot.

   Although there had been complaints to the reigning pope, Eugenius
III, about Breakspear's administration, he was nevertheless made
Bishop of Alba, with the special task of converting Denmark and
Norway, where he displayed considerable skill in uniting the clergy. On
Pope Eugenius's death, Breakspear was elected to fill the vacancy. He
has been described as a mild man with a kindly bearing, respected for

The tablet to Adrian IV in Abbots Langley church

AT BEDMOND IN THIS PARISH
ABOUT THE DATE OF THE
BUILDING OF THIS PRESENT CHURCH
WAS BORN NICHOLAS BREAKSPEAR
POPE ADRIAN IV (1154-1159) THE ONLY
ENGLISH POPE
THIS TABLET IS ERECTED
BY THE HERTFORDSHIRE HISTORICAL
ASSOCIATION · · 1924

his high character and learning; and he was an excellent preacher with a fine voice.

Breakspear accepted the pontificate with reluctance, because of the struggles and difficulties which then beset the Church. But he soon won a reputation for being resolute, skilful and decisive.

A notable event in his tour as Pope was, it is claimed, granting Ireland to Henry II on the ground that all islands converted to Christianity belonged to the Holy See.

The cause of Pope Adrian's death is uncertain. He is said to have choked on a fly or been poisoned.

Places of Interest in the Neighbourhood
    Buried in the 'Wrong' Tomb (Kings Langley)
    The Plague Door (Sarratt)
    Charlie Chaplin Played Here (Watford)

Aldenham Church, with its puddingstone tower

2 A Tower of 'Pudding'

Position: Aldenham, east of Watford.
O.S. Map: Luton & Hertford area; Sheet 166; 1/50,000.
Map Ref: TQ 140/985.
Access: Aldenham is about a mile east of Watford. Take the B462 east towards Radlett and turn off left.

Aldenham Church's 13th-century tower contains large chunks of a rare natural rock called 'puddingstone' – found almost exclusively in Hertfordshire. A close look reveals many pieces of it, cut into shape and used for facing. And in the churchyard, the tomb of a local benefactor, Robert Charles Phillimore, who died in 1919, and his wife Lucy (d. 1957) is made entirely of this stone.

Great boulders of Hertfordshire puddingstone, sometimes as much as eight feet across, can be seen lying about in various parts of the county – on village greens or roadsides. But lapidarists use small pieces of it for ornaments and jewellery, as it is capable of taking a high polish. It is also very hard. The Romans, ever resourceful, used it in their homes for rotary querns – millstones for grinding corn – and whetstones (there are examples of these in Verulamium Museum, in St Albans). But it has been most frequently used as a building material, particularly in church walls.

Puddingstone is so called because of its resemblance to plum pudding. It is a conglomerate made up of coloured flint pebbles – black, brown, red, yellow, pink and orange – up to two inches across, set in a hard natural silica cement called matrix. It was formed 60 million years ago from the pebble beds which were deposited when the sea withdrew from south-east England. When the sea returned, it brought with it material that produced the 'cement'. Then the beds rose to form dry land.

Archaeologists have been surprised that dowsing rods react to puddingstone as they do to water – and no-one can explain why.

Places of Interest in the Neighbourhood
  The Poet who Rebuked the Kaiser (Bushey)
  Overnight Stop for Wrongdoers (Shenley)
  Charlie Chaplain Played Here (Watford)

3 Lament of the Black Death

Position: Ashwell, north-east of Baldock.
O.S. Map: Bedford & Huntingdon area, Sheet 153; 1:50,000.
Map Ref: TL 267/398.
Access: Ashwell Church is off the A1 (T), 4 miles NE of Stotfold.

The lavish size of the beautiful church of St Mary the Virgin in Ashwell, in the far north of the county, indicates the prosperity of the village in the 14th century, when it was built. But inside are poignant reminders of Ashwell's sufferings, too – from plague – the first of several curiosities here.

The Black Death first hit Ashwell in the summer of 1349. A year or so later, an obviously educated inhabitant – probably a monk, or other cleric – carved a sad comment in Latin on the north wall of the tower: *'M.C.T (er) x penta miseranda ferox violenta (discessit pestis) superest plebs pessima testis in fine q e vent(us) (erat) valid(us) (...h)oc anno maurus in orbe tonat MCCCLXI* (1000, three times 100, five times 10) a pitable, fierce violent (plague departed); a wretched populace survives to witness (the plague) and in the end a mighty wind, Maurus, thunders in this year in the world 1361'.

The inscription, one of a number in the church, is clearly visible, along with a drawing thought to be of the predecessor of Sir Christopher Wren's St Paul's Cathedral – the old Gothic one. It is the most important of the drawings here, not simply because of its subject, but because detailed medieval drawings of buildings are rare.

Black Death graffiti in Ashwell Church

The old Guild House, with its pargeted front, and the date 1681

In the centre of the High Street, next to St John's Guild Hall (c. 1476) notice the old Guild House, whose façade displays a fine example of 'pargeting' – decorative plasterwork typical of this part of Hertfordshire and across the border into Essex – with the date 1681.

Within a stone's throw of the Three Tuns Hotel, at the junction of Station Road and Springhead (map ref: TL 270/397) are the springs that give the town its name (springs were called 'wells' in Saxon times). Look down from the roadside and see water bubbling out of the natural chalk – for the statistically minded, a million and a third gallons of it a day. This is the source of the river Rhee, and the spring water follows along to the rivers Cam and then Ouse, finally reaching the sea at the Wash 65 miles away.

The springs are an officially designated Site of Special Scientific Interest, for among the fauna are two species of fresh-water flatworm: *Crenobia alpina* and *Polycelis felina*. These are known as 'relicts' – creatures that have survived from another age, in this case the Ice Age.

Places of Interest in the Neighbourhood
Pepys Deciphered (Baldock)
The Clutterbuck Connection (Hinxworth)
The Enigma of the Cave (Royston)

4 Bernard Shaw's 'Dell and Dwelling'

Position: Ayot St Lawrence, near Wheathampstead.
O.S. Map: Luton & Hertford area; Sheet 166; 1:50,000.
Map Ref: TL 194/167
Access: Shaw's Corner stands at the junction of Bibbs Hall Lane and
Bride Hall Lane, in the village.

Shaw's Corner, once the home of the playwright George Bernard Shaw,
is frozen in time, along with its contents. When he died in 1950 he left
instructions that everything in the house, which is stocked with
memorabilia and personal belongings, should remain as it was. And the
National Trust, into whose hands the house has passed, has obeyed his
wishes. Although Shaw was an Irishman, he cherished Ayot St
Lawrence, where he lived for 44 years.

At Shaw's Corner, which is open to the public during the summer,
Shaw wrote, among many other famous works, Pygmalion and Saint
Joan. Visitors come from all over the world to see the study where he
worked, along with all his books and writing equipment and private
treasures; the drawing room where he received his guests; the dining
room where he lingered too long over his meals (to the chagrin of his
housekeeper, Mrs Alice Laden); his bedroom, bathroom, kitchen - and

George Bernard Shaw's desk at Shaw's Corner

the hall, where his hatstand is still adorned with many varieties of headgear. The soft homburg there is at least 60 years old.

Visiting Shaw's kitchen brings back memories for me, for I have a personal interest in Shaw's Corner. It was in 1945, as a naive 17-year-old, when I cycled out to Shaw to seek his advice on entering journalism. Shaw, who was entertaining a guest in the garden on that warm Saturday afternoon, said, with characteristic brusqueness: 'Well, now you've seen the animal, you'd better go.' I did, but not before enjoying tea, treacle tart and a talk with his housekeeper, Mrs Laden, in the kitchen. Later, Shaw sent me a handwritten – and helpful – postcard, and later still there came what amounted to an apology. 'I was not intentionally disagreeable,' he wrote.

Visitors can tour Shaw's pleasant garden, at the bottom of which is his wooden revolving summerhouse. Here he often liked to work in seclusion, insulated from interruption. On or around Shaw's birthday (July 26th) performances of his works are given in the garden. Shaw wrote in his affectionate and witty 'Rhyming Picture Guide' to the village – his last work:

> This is my dell, and this my dwelling,
> Their charm so far beyond my telling,
> That though in Ireland is my birthplace,
> This house shall be my final earthplace.

... as indeed it became. He died there at the age of 94, and his ashes were scattered in the garden.

Places of Interest in the Neighbourhood
  Divided in Death (Ayot St Lawrence)
  That Wicked Lady (Wheathampstead)
  Where Old Battles Were Fought (Wheathampstead)

5 Divided in Death

Position: Ayot St Lawrence, near Wheathampstead.
O.S. Map: Luton & Hertford area; Sheet 166; 1:50,000.
Map Ref: TL 192/169.
Access: To reach the new church, take the path for a few hundred yards from Ayot St Lawrence village, 2 miles west of Welwyn.

In 1775, because it spoiled his view from Ayot House, which stands to the north of it, Sir Lyonel Lyde began to demolish the old church of St Lawrence – now a forlorn but picturesque ruin in the village. When demolition removed the roof and many of the timbers, news reached the Bishop of Lincoln (in whose diocese, surprisingly, the church stood), and he prevented further destruction by issuing an injunction.

A footpath runs westwards across the fields from the old church to the 'new' Church of St Lawrence, designed and built in 1778 in the classical style of Nicholas Revett. Sir Lyonel had it built, partly to serve as a trompe l'oeil from the house, and partly as a replacement for the old church.

It seems, however, that Sir Lyonel and Lady Lyde did not enjoy a happy marriage. Thus, at opposite ends of the new church's colonnade are two pavilions; in one lie the remains of Sir Lyonel, and in the other those of Lady Lyde. Sir Lyonel promised that the church which united them in life should divide them in death.

But the church, still in regular use, is otherwise a picture of perfect Palladian-style harmony.

Places of Interest in the Neighbourhood
  Bernard Shaw's 'Dell and Dwelling' (Ayot St Lawrence)
  That Wicked Lady (Wheathampstead)
  Where Old Battles were Fought (Wheathampstead)

The 'new' church at Ayot St Lawrence

6 Pepys Deciphered

Position: Baldock.
O.S. Map: Luton & Hertford area; Sheet 166; 1:50,000.
Map Ref: TL 245/339.
Access: Baldock church is near junction of Hitchin Street (A505) and Church Street in the town centre.

Early last century, the Rev John Smith, who is buried with his wife in the churchyard at the eastern end of this fine, tall-spired church, became famous as an undergraduate. While studying at St John's College, Cambridge, he gave himself the task of deciphering all six volumes of shorthand (3,000 pages) comprising Pepys's diaries, which had lain for nearly a century in Pepys's library at Magdalene. Mr Smith, the future Rector of Baldock (from 1832 to 1870), spent three years transcribing them all into longhand.

But, feat as it undoubtedly was, this was a labour of love largely wasted. For, unbeknown to Smith, there was a small book in Pepys's library that could have saved Smith much of his labour. Charles II had dictated to Pepys an account of his escape after the Battle of Worcester – and there was a longhand translation of the shorthand which held the key to the Pepys's entire diary.

Places of Interest in the Neighbourhood
    Sir Ebenezer's Dream (Letchworth)
    Miss Lawrence's 'Folly' (Letchworth)
    George Orwell's Shop (Wallington)

7 A Gift of Milestones

Position: Barkway, south-east of Royston.
O.S. Map: Cambridge & Newmarket; Sheet 154; 1:50,000.
Map Ref: TL 385/358.
Access: Milestone is in High St at the north end of the village; outside
Barkway House.

Along what was once a turnpike road to Cambridge is an interesting
milestone – one of a number erected by two Fellows of Trinity College,
Cambridge, in around 1725 to indicate the way to the city.

The milestone stands about five feet high. It is the most southerly and
the most decorative of the 15 milestones between Cambridge and
Barkway – there are others northwards along the B1358 through
Barley. They were paid for from a fund set up for the purpose by the
two Fellows, Dr Mouse and Robert Hare.

Places of Interest in the Neighbourhood
   A Sign of the Chase (Barley)
   Tomb of a Dragon Killer (Brent Pelham)
   The Enigma of the Cave (Royston)

The milestone gift at Barkway

8 Sign of the Chase

Position: Barley, south-east of Royston.
O.S. Map: Cambridge & Newmarket area; Sheet 154; 1:50,000.
Map Ref: TL 396/382.
Access: The Fox and Hounds Inn is on the B1039 east of the village.

In this beautiful village in the extreme north-east of the county stands the Fox and Hounds Inn, which was converted from a farmhouse in 1797 but dates from the 15th century. Its claim to fame is its 'gallows' sign, which features painted figures of huntsmen, hounds and fox, and stretches the full width of Church End, on which the inn stands, on the road to Saffron Walden.

Such signs are a rarity. What makes this one even rarer is that it originally belonged to another Fox and Hounds – a few hundred yards along the road - which was burnt down in 1950. The sign survived the fire, and the present Fox and Hounds (formerly the Waggon & Horses) acquired it, and changed its name to match the sign!

Places of Interest in the Neighbourhood
A Gift of Milestones (Barkway)
Tomb of a Dragon Killer (Brent Pelham)
The Enigma of the Cave (Royston)

The rare Fox and Hounds inn sign at Barley

9 Where Warwick the Kingmaker Died

Position: Hadley Highstone, on the northern fringe of Barnet.
O.S. Map: Luton & Hertford area; Sheet 166; 1:50,000.
Map ref: TQ 247/981.
Access: The obelisk is in a fork where Kitts End Road joins the A1000 (Gt North Road) north of Hadley Green.

This stone, on the site of the Battle of Barnet, fought on April 14th, 1471, was erected in 1740 by Sir Jeremy Sambrooke (see 'Gateway to Nowhere'). The battle, one of many in the Wars of the Roses, was between the Yorkist army under Edward IV and the Lancastrians commanded by the Earl of Warwick (Warwick the Kingmaker).

The battle lines were drawn up across what is today the A1000. Warwick himself commanded the Lancastrians' left flank. Opposite him, on the Barnet side, were the Yorkists, whose right flank was commanded by a man to become notorious a little later in history, Richard of Gloucester. He became Richard III, and died on Bosworth Field, near Leicester, in the last battle of the Wars of the Roses in 1485.

During the three or four hours of fighting at Barnet, about 1,500 lives were lost, including that of Warwick the Kingmaker himself. It is widely thought that he died in the immediate vicinity of the obelisk. With Warwick's death, medieval England lost one of its leading and most colourful figures: politician, courtier, soldier – courageous in battle, admired for his many qualities, and to the people of England a hero.

Places of Interest in the Neighbourhood
'Customs' Posts for Coal (Brookmans Park)
An Ancient Beacon (Monken Hadley)
A War Leader's Last Resting-place (Ridge)

The obelisk at Hadley, marking the Battle of Barnet

10 Dr Dimsdale, Russian Baron

Position: Between Hertford and Bengeo.
O.S. Map: Luton & Hertford area; Sheet 166; 1/50,000.
Map Ref: TL 320/137.
Access: Take B158 (Port Hill) towards Bengeo. After three-quarters of
a mile turn left into Cross Road, follow the private road opposite, at the
end of which is Port Hill House. (Not accessible to the public – to be
seen only from the drive gate.)

In this house, Dr Thomas Dimsdale, a remarkable 18th-century
physician who became rich through his own medical knowledge and the
generous patronage of Russian royalty, had his clinic and 'inoculating
house'. Humanity owes a great debt to his pioneering expertise, for it is
thanks largely to him and his fellow doctors that smallpox, a virulent
disease during his lifetime with a 30 per cent fatality rate, has been
almost entirely wiped out.

Dr Dimsdale, who was born in 1712 and was a Quaker, began to
practise in Hertford in around 1734; he lived in the Priory in Hertford
town, and in 1762 bought Port Hill House for a mere £60 to use as a
clinic. And at the foot of the garden he had an isolation hospital built
for victims of contagious diseases, including smallpox, which yielded

Dr Dimsdale's Old Pest House, Bengeo

material for his inoculations at Port Hill. It was called the Pest House, and the name survives. The Old Pest House is a private house on the corner of Fanshawe and Byde Streets (visible from the road but not open to the public).

Fame came after 1767, when the doctor wrote a treatise, 'The Present Method of Inoculating for the Smallpox', which ran to many editions. Through his inoculations, news of Dr Dimsdale's work spread throughout Europe, and eventually to Russia. In 1768 he was invited to St Petersburg by the Empress Catherine to inoculate herself and her son, the Grand Duke Paul. As a precaution – in case the inoculation was not a success and roused the ire of her subjects – she had a series of post-horses waiting to ease his escape from the country.

However, the project was a success, and the rewards were considerable all round. Dr Dimsdale was made a councillor of state, received the hereditary title of Baron of the Russian Empire and with it a bounty of £10,000, £2,000 expenses and an annuity of £500 – huge sums in those days. He was also given the right to incorporate a wing of the imperial Russian eagle into his family coat of arms.

In 1769 he was given a black Siberian fox fur muff (which apparently the royal family were privileged to wear) belonging to the Empress. Dimsdale returned to Russia in 1781 (by this time he was MP for Hertford), and inoculated the Grand Duke Alexander and his brother Constantine.

The Dimsdale coat-of-arms can be seen on the sign of the Dimsdale Arms Hotel (78 Fore Street, Hertford), which until the 1920s was owned by Dr Dimsdale's descendants, some of whom still live in Hertfordshire. There is a motto underneath, not part of the original coat-of-arms, which reads 'Magnus Hippocrates tu nobis major': 'Hippocrates was great; to us, you are greater'.

Places of Interest in the Neighbourhood
Fox's Ancient Chair (Hertford)
Kings of the Castle (Hertford)
A Poet's 'Fairy Palace' (Ware)

Dr Dimsdale

11 Meeting Place of Kings

Position: Benington, east of Stevenage.
O.S. Map: Luton & Hertford area; Sheet 166; 1/50,000.
Map Ref: TL 298/237.
Access: The Lordship is next to the village green, which is to the east of the church path.

In Benington, in one of the county's pleasantest villages, stands Benington Lordship, an estate which spans history from Saxon times. It is situated in idyllic gardens, and is early Georgian; but it stands on the site of a Norman castle whose crumbling remains, half obscured by wandering foliage, can still be seen, along with the moat and bailey. The Norman keep, a Grade I listed monument, was built 10 years after the

castle and is claimed to be the only example of vernacular Norman architecture in the county. The castle was built in 1128 and finally demolished in 1212. But the gatehouse, which adjoins the house, impressive as it is, is merely a folly, built in 1832.

Even the Normans are pre-dated here. On the site of the Lordship – lordship being another name for manor house – was the seat of the Saxon kings of Mercia, and in 850 AD one of them, Bertulf, held a council here to discuss reports that the Danes had captured Canterbury and London, and that their fleet was in the Thames. But he failed to stop their advance.

The manor house, an imposing building of red brick, is early 18th century, but there was a manor here 500 years earlier. John de Benstede, its owner from 1285, is buried in a tomb in the neighbouring 700-year-old church of St Peter, which is set back from the village and whose tower is just the other side of the wall from Benington Lordship grounds.

The gardens are open every year between February and August.

Places of Interest in the Neighbourhood
  Sir Edward's Stately Fantasy (Knebworth)
  Dick Turpin's Getaway (Stevenage)
  The Witch Who Never Was (Walkern)

12 Where the Saxons Surrendered

Position: Berkhamsted, west of Hemel Hempstead.
O.S. Map: Aylesbury & Leighton Buzzard area; Sheet 165; 1/50,000.
Map Ref: SP 997/083.
Access: For the castle, go down Lower King's Rd, off the High Street, past the railway station on left, through arch into Whitehill.

It is possible to walk completely round the outer bailey of the remains of Berkhamsted Castle – which allows plenty of time to contemplate the event that took place here. This castle was the scene of a historic surrender. Two months after his victory over King Harold at Hastings, William the Conqueror set about encircling London. Realising that London could not be defended by the English, a deputation of Saxon nobles assembled to meet William at Berkhamsted, to offer him the throne of England. William promised to be a 'kind lord' to them.

The castle went to William's half-brother, Robert of Montain, and it is his work on the earthworks of the motte-and-bailey castle that can seen today, along with ruined walls of the stone castle built by Thomas Becket, when he was Henry II's Chancellor.

Here, at various times, lived Queen Isabella, wife of King John of France, a prisoner here after the battle of Poitiers in 1356; and Edward the Black Prince, who regarded it as his favourite home and spent his last days here.

The poet Geoffrey Chaucer was Clerk of Works at Berkhamsted Castle in 1389.

Places of Interest in the Neighbourhood
  The Canal Duke (Little Gaddesden)
  The Silent Zoo (Tring)

13 An Empire Builder's House

Position: Bishop's Stortford.
O.S. Map: Chelmsford & Harlow area; Sheet 167; 1/50,000.
Map Ref: TL 492/204.
Access: Rhodes's house, which is open to the public, stands on the east side of South Road.

Empire-building is no longer fashionable, but in this fine early 19th-century semi-detached house, one of the great pioneers of the British Empire was born, in 1853: Cecil Rhodes, statesman, adventurer and diamond tycoon.

The Rhodes family was much respected locally. Cecil was the seventh child of the Vicar of St Michael's, Bishop's Stortford, and his early education was at the local grammar school. Later, he studied at Oriel College, Oxford (of which there is a model on show here). He lived in Bishop's Stortford until he was 17.

The house has now become the Rhodes Memorial Museum and Commonwealth Centre. The bedroom where Rhodes was born has been

The bust of Cecil Rhodes in the Rhodes Memorial Museum, Bishop's Stortford

preserved, and is furnished as it would have been at the time. It contains his Bible, his father's Prayer Book and a letter written by his mother. A number of rooms can be toured, and these contain about 250 photographs, pictures, documents, maps and contemporary newspaper cuttings concerning Rhodes. There are also scores of items of memorabilia from South Africa.

Rhodes made a fortune in diamonds, and there are some remarkable photographs of the Kimberley mines, where hundreds of small claimants worked. Rhodes succeeded in amalgamating their wasteful efforts, becoming one of the founders of the De Beers corporation. Photographs show the 1,300ft deep 'big hole' at Kimberley, which was a mile round the perimeter and which yielded up a total of three tons of diamonds (14 million carats) before being abandoned to become a massive feature of the town – the biggest man-made hole in the world.

In 1889 Rhodes formed the British South Africa Company, occupying lands to form Rhodesia, the forerunner of Zambia and Zimbabwe. He exhausted himself attempting to achieve his dream of a federated South Africa with British, Boers and Blacks under the British flag. But much worked against him, including a Matabele rising and the hostility of the Boers which erupted in the Boer War.

Rhodes died in 1902 at the age of 49. Rudyard Kipling, who was a contemporary of Rhodes, wrote a poem to him, which was read at the funeral. It included the lines:

> Dreamer devout, by vision led
> Beyond our guess or reach,
> The travail of his spirit bred
> Cities in place of speech.
> So huge the all-mastering thought that drove –
> So brief the term allowed –
> Nations not words he linked to prove
> His faith before the crowd.

Rhodes is buried far from his native town – in one of the places that inspired him: the Matopo Hills in Zimbabwe. Another much-valued and abiding memorial is the Rhodes scholarships, created under his will, which enable students from the Commonwealth, the USA and Germany to study at Oxford.

Places of Interest in the Neighbourhood
Man and Nature in Bronze (Perry Green)
The Church with a Detached Tower (Standon)
Dick Whittington, Lord of the Manor (Thorley)

14 Tomb of a Dragon-killer

Position: Brent Pelham, north-west of Bishop's Stortford.
O.S. Map: Chelmsford & Harlow area; Sheet 167; 1/50,000.
Map Ref: TL 433/308.
Access: Take B1038 from A10; Brent Pelham church is to the left of
T-junction in the centre of the village.

If dragons did not exist, then old Piers Shonks, a dragon-slayer at the
time of William the Conqueror, deserved to be made redundant. But
according to tradition he earned his title.

Shonks, a lord of a subordinate manor in the parish of Brent
Pelham, near the Essex border, soon after the Conquest, was buried in
1086 in a strange tomb set in the north wall of Brent Pelham church.
The top of the tomb is covered with an old slab of Petworth marble, in
high relief, with the figure of an angel, and sustaining a festoon of
drapery, out of which rises a small human figure, with his hands raised
in prayer, and a fire-breathing dragon.

It seems there was a notorious local dragon, which lived in a cave
under a yew tree – a dragon favoured by the Devil. Because it was
causing so much distress, Shonks donned armour, armed himself with
sword and spear, took with him a servant and three hounds, and killed
it. This exploit so angered the Devil that he swore to have Piers Shonks
'body and soul, whether buried within the church or out'. But Shonks's
relatives and friends sidestepped this threat by burying him neither
inside nor outside the church, but in an alcove in the solid wall.

This inscription, probably dating from the 18th century, appears on
the wall behind the tomb:

> Nothing of Cadmus, or St George, those names
> Of great renown, survives them, but their fame;
> Time was so sharp set as to make no bones
> Of theirs, nor of their monumental stones.
> But Shonke one serpent kills, t'other defies,
> And in this wall, as in a fortress, lies.

When Shonks's tomb was opened in 1861, they found large bones
inside. This has given rise to speculation that Shonks was a giant. In the
Middle Ages, of course, there were a lot of them about. Dragons, too,
apparently.

Places of Interest in the Neighbourhood
    A Picture in Brass (Buntingford)
    Warning of the Gunpowder Plot (Furneux Pelham)

15 Home of Miss Muffet?

Position: Brookmans Park, north of Potters Bar.
O.S. Map: Luton & Hertford area; Sheet 166; 1/50,000.
Map Ref: TL 250/041.
Access: Moffats Farm, in Moffats Lane, is a private house, and
although visible from the road is not open to the public.

There is a legendary connection between Little Miss Muffet of the
nursery rhyme and this house. Dorothy Colville, in her book, *North
Mymms – People and Parish*, notes that a Dr Thomas Muffett, an
entomologist who died in 1604, had an admiration for spiders that has
'never been surpassed'. He is said to have written the 'Little Miss
Muffet' verse after an encounter with a spider by his small daughter
Patience. The poem did not appear in print until 1805, in an American
book, *Songs for the Nursery*.

But doubts have grown about the story that Dr Moffat lived here.
Because Moffat's was built in 1662, 58 years after the doctor's death, it
is reckoned that a likelier candidate was Moffats Farm, 100 yards or so
down the Moffats Lane and built in the 16th century.

Places of Interest in the Neighbourhood
   'Customs' Posts for Coal (Brookmans Park)
   Night of the Zeppelin (Cuffley)
   Gateway to Nowhere (North Mymms)

The coal post in Brookmans Park

16 'Customs' Posts for Coal

Position: Brookmans Park, north of Potters Bar.
O.S. Map: Luton & Hertford area; Sheet 166; 1/50,000.
Map Ref: TL 271/034.
Access: The coal post is at the junction of Well Road, Shepherds Way and The Ridgeway, near Queenswood School.

This is one of around 36 'coalposts' scattered across the south of the county between Wormley and Rickmansworth to mark London's ancient customs boundary. They are made of stone, granite or cast iron, and most of them bear the Corporation's coat-of-arms - a shield containing the cross of St George and a sword in one quarter.

The purpose of the posts is rooted in the 17th century, when the City was empowered to levy duty on coal and wine entering the London area. The tax's yield helped to contribute to the cost of rebuilding work after the Great Fire of London and the Plague.

The posts were renewed, and their position shifted, several times under successive legislation. The mark '14 & 15 Vic' or '24 Vic' on them indicates the year of the statute empowering them during Queen Victoria's reign, which began in 1837. So the mark '24 Vic' indicates the year 1861.

The benefits to London of the huge revenues raised were said to be immense: they helped the City to restore 50 City streets, rebuild more than 50 churches, erect St Paul's Cathedral, Guildhall and the Old Bailey, restore Westminster Abbey and build the Albert Embankment and Holborn Viaduct.

In theory, the Corporation still looks after the posts, even though coal and wine duties ceased in 1897. But many of the posts, two or three of which can be seen in the vicinity of Potters Bar and Colney Heath, are neglected.

Places of Interest in the Neighbourhood
   Home of Miss Muffet? (Brookman's Park)
   Night of the Zeppelin (Cuffley)
   Gateway to Nowhere (North Mymms)

17 A Picture in Brass

Position: Buntingford, north-east of Stevenage.
O.S. Map: Luton & Hertford area; Sheet 166; 1:50,000.
Map Ref: TL 363/292.
Access: St Peter's church is in Buntingford High Street, near the junction with the B1038.

One of the most unusual among around 200 figure brasses in the county is also one of the smallest and most detailed. It is in the church of St Peter, which was built between 1614 and 1626 as a chapel-of-ease to the nearby village of Layston. St Peter's is supposed to be the earliest purpose-built Anglican church made of brick in the country.

The brass plate, 37cm x 25 cm and dated 1620, hangs on the south wall as a memorial to the then incumbent, Alexander Strange, and shows him preaching to the congregation from his canopied pulpit, with windows in the background. It is all in such minute detail that a magnifying glass is needed to distinguish it.

Places of Interest in the Neighbourhood
   Tomb of a Dragon Killer (Brent Pelham)
   A Warning of the Gunpowder Plot (Furneux Pelham)
   The Church with a Detached Tower (Standon)

18   The Poet Who Rebuked the Kaiser

Position: Bushey, south-east of Watford.
O.S. Map: Luton & Hertford area; Sheet 166; 1/50,000.
Map Ref: TQ 129/953.
Access: The churchyard lies back from the High Street. Pain's grave is a few yards to the right of the main door.

Buried in Bushey churchyard is Barry Pain, a novelist, parodist and poet (1864-1928), who wrote one of the most famous poems of World War I. He delivered a strong rebuke – in verse – to the Kaiser, who had asserted, in a telegraphed message, that God had magnificently supported the Germans. The end of the poem read as follows:

> Impious braggart, you forget,
> God is not your conscript yet;
> You shall learn in dumb amaze
> That His ways are not your ways,
> That the mire through which you trod
> Is not the high white road of God.
>
> To Whom, whichever way the combat rolls,
> We, fighting to the end, commend our souls.

Pain was born in Cambridge, and lived for a few years in Hogarth House, Bushey, until about 1908. He died at Watford. His poetic address to the Kaiser was interesting because much of his work, including his novels, was humorous, though he had been advised by the writer W. E. Henley that he should concentrate on being 'serious'.

Barry Pain had many talents and wide interests, including drawing, Georgian literature, occult lore and precious stones. As well as poetry, his literary output included a philosophic religious treatise and a detective novel and stories of the supernatural.

For a time Pain served in the First World War in the anti-aircraft section of the RNVR, serving at the searchlight station on Parliament Hill, London.

Places of Interest in the Neighbourhood
   Birthplace of England's Only Pope (Abbots Langley)
   A Tower of 'Pudding' (Aldenham)
   Charlie Chaplin Played Here (Watford)

19 A Lamb Legacy

Position: North-east of Cherry Green, near Puckeridge.
O.S. Map: Luton & Hertford area; Sheet 166; 1/50,000.
Map Ref: TL 349/265.
Access: For Button Snap, turn left off the A10(M) at Puckeridge; after two miles, turn right at Gt Munden to Cherry Green.

The essayist Charles Lamb was a lover of Hertfordshire, and this solitary whitewashed thatched cottage near Cherry Green, called Button Snap – a legacy from his godfather – would no doubt have contributed to his pleasures.

But, strangely, although he refers to it in the essay, 'My First Play', there is no real evidence that he actually lived there. 'When I journeyed down to take possession,' he wrote, 'and planted my foot on my own ground, the stately habits of the donor descended upon me, and I strode (shall I confess the vanity?) with larger paces over my allotment of three quarters of an acre, with its commodious mansion in the midst, with the feeling of an English freeholder that all betwixt sky and centre was my own.'

Button Snap is privately owned and can be seen only from the road. (see 'Essayist's Holiday Home'.)

Places of Interest in the Neighbourhood
   Meeting Place of Kings (Benington)
   A Picture in Brass (Buntingford)
   The Church with a Detached Tower (Standon)

Button Snap, which belonged to Charles Lamb

20 Wren's Banished Gateway

Position: Theobalds Park, Cheshunt.
O.S. Map: Luton & Hertford area; Sheet 166; 1/50,000.
Map Ref: TL 344/010.
Access: Temple Bar is along a narrow road from the B198, off the A10

Temple Bar, the venerable – and decaying – monument which stands
neglected in this southern corner of Hertfordshire, once had a nobler

Temple Bar, one-time gateway to the City of London

role. Designed by Sir Christopher Wren, it served as the western gateway to the City of London, dominating the confluence of Fleet Street and the Strand between 1672 and 1878, when it was dismantled. This was because Temple Bar's centre arch was inadequate to handle the increasing London traffic, a situation worsened by the building of the new Law Courts to the west of it.

Temple Bar is built in what has been called English Renaissance style. Beneath the large curved pediment are four larger than lifesize effigies – two each on the front and rear elevations: of Charles I and II on one side, and James I (who once owned Theobalds, where Temple Bar now stands) and his wife Queen Anne of Denmark on the other. Either side of the large central arch are two other arches, used by pedestrians when the Bar stood in the Strand.

The monument was designed and built for £1,500 by Wren when he was Surveyor-General of the Royal Works to Charles II. Every one of its 2,000 pieces was hewn, like those of St Paul's Cathedral, from Portland stone.

Many people in the county, saddened by the condition of Temple Bar and the fact of its banishment, have fought to have it returned to the City. Certainly not back in Fleet Street, but perhaps next to Wren's greatest glory, St Paul's Cathedral.

Places of Interest in the Neighbourhood
    The King and the Tinker (Cheshunt)
    Last Journey of a Queen (Waltham Cross)

The sign at the King and Tinker

21   The King and the Tinker

Position: Cheshunt.
O.S. Map: Luton & Hertford; Sheet 166; 1/50,000.
Map Ref: TL 330/998.
Access: The King & Tinker inn is in Whitewebbs Lane, about 2 miles east of Crews Hill station (BR)

The porch is the oldest part of the attractive King and Tinker inn, which is claimed to have originated around 1,000 years ago, and according to tradition it was here that a celebrated meeting of King James I and a tinker took place. The story is that one day, returning from hunting, King James left his party and went off to seek adventure on his own. He found it at the inn. Here he met a tinker, 'spoke to him in sportive mood' and called for a pitcher of ale. The tinker stood his round and bought him one in return.

One report is that the tinker's conversation so pleased the King that he knighted him. An old ballad describes the incident:

> 'Come! Tell me thy name.' ' I am John of the Dale,
> A mender of kettles, and a lover of good ale.'
> 'Then rise up, Sir John, for I'll honour thee here,
> I make thee a Knight of five hundred a year....'

King James had a palace at nearby Theobalds. He had been so impressed with the place, having spent a night there on his way to London to be crowned, that he persuaded Sir Robert Cecil, who lived there, to exchange it for the royal manor of Hatfield. The king regularly hunted in nearby Enfield Chase, as Queen Elizabeth I did before him. He died at Theobalds in 1625.

Places of Interest in the Neighbourhood
   Wren's Banished Gateway (Cheshunt)
   Last Journey of a Queen (Waltham Cross)

22   A Public House with Punch

Position: Chipperfield, north-west of Watford.
O.S. Map: Luton & Hertford area; Sheet 166; 1/50,000.
Map Ref: TL 043/016.
Access: The Two Brewers Inn overlooks Chipperfield Common.

In Victorian times, the thud of fists on flesh was a familiar sound at the Two Brewers, in contrast to its peaceful demeanour today. For this was a training retreat for some of the leading pugilists, among them Jem Mace and Tom Sayers. (Also claimed to have trained there is Bob Fitzsimmons, who was born in Cornwall and was the only Englishman to win the world heavyweight championship under Queensberry Rules, though it seems unlikely as he went abroad at the age of two and eventually became a U.S. citizen. He beat 'Gentleman' Jim Corbett in America in 1897.)

   The early boxers' 'gym' was the clubroom at the back of the inn, and spectators went from miles around to watch them in action. Local boys, seeing their heroes on training runs round the common, were sometimes inspired to try their luck in the ring with the champions.

Places of Interest in the Neighbourhood
   Birthplace of England's Only Pope (Abbots Langley)
   Buried in the 'Wrong' Tomb (Kings Langley)
   Charlie Chaplin Played Here (Watford)

The Gardens of the Rose, Chiswell Green

23 Roses, Roses All the Way

Position: At Bone Hill, three-quarters of a mile east of Chiswell Green,
south-west of St Albans.
O.S. Map: Luton & Hertford area; Sheet 166; 1/50,000.
Map Ref: TL 124/045.
Access: The Gardens of the Rose are reached from M1 (junction 6)
and M25 (junction 21a).

The 12 acres of the Gardens of the Rose offer the dazzling spectacle of
one of the most important collections of roses in the world: 30,000 in
1,700 varieties. This is the the headquarters of the Royal National Rose
Society, Britain's oldest and biggest specialist horticultural society.

But statistics, impressive as they are, cannot describe the beguiling
scents that assail visitors wandering the length and breadth of these
colourful acres, for more than five months of the year. Among the
historical cultivated roses you can see are the Gallicas, or French roses.
R. gallica 'Officinalis', the Apothecary's Rose, is thought to be the Red
Rose of Lancaster in the Wars of the Roses; likewise R. x alba
Semi-plena, the White Rose of York. In fact, the roses at the Gardens of
the Rose span history up to the present day.

All the various kinds of rose are represented: large-flowered (hybrid
tea), cluster flowered (floribunda), climbers, shrub roses old and new,
miniatures, and the latest development, the ground-cover rose for both
large and small gardens.

Methods of display are also demonstrated in a series of small
gardens, so that roses can be adapted to one's own plot. One of the
most spectacular areas is the pergola and pool, showing climbing roses
and clematis grown in association on no fewer than 46 brick pillars.

Besides being beautiful to see, the gardens do of course have a
serious horticultural function. In the trial grounds, new roses come
from all over the world to be rigorously assessed over a three-year
period for their value as garden plants.

The highlight of the year at Bone Hill is the British Rose Festival,
which is held early in July, when the roses are at the height of their first
flush. The gardens are open to the public from mid-June to late
October.

Places of Interest in the Neighbourhood
  Playhouse of the Legions (St Albans)
  The Inn that was Once a Cockpit (St Albans)
  The Violin that Plays Itself (St Albans)

24 Bunyan's Chimney

Position: Coleman Green hamlet, three miles NE of St Albans.
O.S. Map: Luton & Hertford area; Sheet 166; 1/50,000.
Map Ref: TL 191/127.
Access: The chimney stands in an enclosure beside the Roman road which runs through the hamlet. It is about 200 yards north-east of the John Bunyan inn.

One of the most bizarre of memorials is this chimney, dedicated to John Bunyan, author of *The Pilgrim's Progress*, who was a familiar figure in these parts. There is an inscription on the chimney high above one's head, but this can be read only with difficulty. 'John Bunyan,' it notes, 'is said by tradition to have preached and occasionally to have lodged in the cottage of which this chimney formed part.'

Bunyan, son of a tinker, Baptist and a former conscript in the Parliamentary army in the Civil War, was imprisoned twice for preaching, much of which he carried out among the peaceful villages of Bedfordshire and Hertfordshire. He was born at Elstow, near Bedford, in 1628, and had written around 60 books by the time he died in 1688.

Places of Interest in the Neighbourhood
   Roses, Roses All the Way (Chiswell Green)
   Playhouse of the Legions (St Albans)
   That Wicked Lady (Wheathampstead)

Bunyan's Chimney, Coleman Green

43

25 Night of the Zeppelin

Position: Cuffley.
O.S. Map: Luton & Hertford area; Sheet 166; 1/50,000.
Map Ref: TL 302/030.
Access: The memorial stands on the B157 (East Ridgeway), a mile west of Cuffley village.

This stone marks the place where, on the night of September 2nd/3rd, 1916, a German 'Zeppelin' was brought down in flames over Cuffley – a spectacle visible all over North London. It was the first German airship to be destroyed on British soil, and paved the way for the abandonment of airships as a strategic weapon. Four British people were killed in the raid and 12 injured, and 16 Germans died.

Zeppelins had hitherto claimed 352 lives. This one was despatched by 19-year-old Lt William Leefe Robinson, flying a BE2c biplane, and using a new kind of explosive bullet. The exploit earned him the first VC for action over Britain for his 'most conspicuous bravery' in attacking the airship in circumstances of great difficulty. He had been in the air for more than two hours, and had previous attacked another German marauder during his flight.

Leefe Robinson, whose exploit is noted on the memorial (subscribed for by readers of *The Daily Express*), served with the Worcester Regt and the Royal Flying Corps.

The airship was not a true Zeppelin (though all German airships were so called by the British), but a Schutte-Lanz airship. It was identified from its use of wood and wire for the inner frame: the true Zeppelin used aluminium. Around 60,000 people flocked to Cuffley to see its remains, and thousands of people took away souvenir pieces of it. The inquest on the German airmen took place in the Plough public house along the road on Plough Hill.

Lt Leefe Robinson's daring made him a national hero. He was taken prisoner in 1917, and when released contracted tuberculosis. He died of flu at the age of 21 and is buried at Stanmore, Middlesex.

Places of Interest in the Neighbourhood
  'Customs' Posts for Coal (Brookmans Park)
  Wren's Vanished Gateway (Cheshunt)
  The King and the Tinker (Cheshunt)

Where the Zeppelin landed: the Cuffley memorial

26 The Frightened Rector

Position: Essendon, east of Hatfield.
O.S. Map: Luton & Hertford area; Sheet 166; 1/50,000.
Map Ref: TL 274/088.
Access: Take A1000 from Potters Bar towards Hatfield, turn right on to the B158 and follow it to Essendon.

In a shady corner of the churchyard of St Mary the Virgin, Essendon's parish church, with its 15th-century tower, is the unprepossessing tomb of a former incumbent, the Rev. Richard Orme, who died in 1843 after being rector for 52 years. The rector was so apprehensive at the possibility of being buried alive that he wanted his tomb above ground. He also insisted that it should have a locked door (there is a steel door at one end), and that he should be buried with the key to the tomb, a bottle of wine, a loaf of bread.

The rector's grave appears to be facing east, along with all the other graves. It used to be the custom for the clergy to face west. This was because, when Judgment Day came, the dead would rise up facing Jerusalem, and all clerics would be in a natural position to address their congregations!

A tablet over the west door notes that a young man convicted of theft in 1785 'begged a grave in this churchyard', and prayed to God that his suffering might prove a warning to others. Another, more recent, plaque, at the eastern end of the church, tells visitors of the bomb damage by the German airship in 1916 (see 'Night of the Zeppelin').

Places of Interest in the Neighbourhood
   A Garden from the Past (Hatfield)
   In Memory of Bishop Ken (Little Berkhamsted)
   The Watchtower that Wasn't (Little Berkhamsted)

27 A Warning of the Gunpowder Plot

Position: Furneux Pelham, east Hertfordshire.
O.S. Map: Chelmsford & Harlow area; Sheet 167; 1/50,000.
Map Ref: TL 427/280.
Access: The Hall is a few hundred yards west of the village.

The clock on Furneux Pelham's 14th-century church urges: 'Time Flies. Mind Your Business' – advice that one local peer wasted no time before taking. For Furneux Pelham Hall, the picturesque 16th-century brick manor house here, was the home of the Catholic Lord Mounteagle, who on October 26th, 1605, received a letter warning him not to attend Parliament, and thus escape the mayhem of the Gunpowder Plot conspirators.

At that time, Catholics were allowed to sit in the House of Lords, and Mounteagle was one of several friends and relatives of the 13 conspirators who received notice of their intention to blow up Parliament. The most famous of them was Guy Fawkes, an explosives expert brought over from Flanders where he had been serving with the Spanish Army.

It was the conspirators' compassion in sending their letter of warning to Mounteagle and his fellow Catholics that in fact betrayed them. The letter read: 'Retire yourself into the country for... they shall receive a terrible blow this Parliament and yet they shall not see who

Furneux Pelham Hall: a link with the Gunpowder Plot

hurts them.'

Mounteagle's sense of duty prompted him to hand over the letter to the Privy Council. As a result, the cellars of Parliament were searched, Fawkes and his fellow conspirators seized, and the Plot foiled.

Furneux Pelham Hall is a handsome house, with stepped and curvilinear gables. It is, however, privately owned, and only the gardens are occasionally open to the public. But the house can be clearly seen from the road.

Places of Interest in the Neighbourhood
  Tomb of a Dragon Killer (Brent Pelham)
  A Lamb Legacy (Cherry Green)
  The Church with a Detached Tower (Standon)

The stone memorial to Sir Hugh Myddelton at Great Amwell

Stone marking the source of the New River, Great Amwell

28 'Father' of the New River

Position: Great Amwell, near Ware.
O.S. Map: Luton & Hertford area; Sheet 166; 1/50,000.
Map Ref: TL 372/125.
Access: Follow A1170 from Hoddesdon to Great Amwell, then turn right down Cautherly Lane, past the George IV public house to a T-junction. The small islands are to the right.

On two small islands in the New River at Great Amwell are stones which commemorate Sir Hugh Myddelton, a man of vision and determination, whose dream it was to provide a badly needed ready supply of water to London. Hence the New River, which snakes for 38 miles from Chadwell Spring (the true source, two miles to the west), Hertford and Amwell, to the Thames below Blackwall, in East London.

A plan along the lines of Sir Hugh's was vaguely formulated in Queen Elizabeth's reign, but not until 1613, thanks largely to help received from James I, was Sir Hugh Myddelton's task completed – despite landowners' greedy demands for outrageous sums in compensation. Sir Hugh invested his own fortune in the project, and was given a well-earned baronetcy in 1622.

On one of the stones appears a poem, but who wrote it is in some doubt. It has been attributed to the Quaker poet John Scott (see 'A Poet's Fairy Palace'), and also to one Archbishop Nares, a friend of the architect and engineer on the New River, Robert Mylne. One verse reads:

> Amwell, perpetual be thy stream
> Nor e'er thy springs be less
> Which thousands drink who never dream
> Whence flows the boon they bless.

The other monument is inscribed: 'From the Spring at Chadwell... and from this source of Amwell the Aqueduct meanders for the space of XL miles conveying health, pleasure and convenience to the metropolis of Gt Britain – an important work since man cannot more nearly imitate the Deity than by bestowing health.'

Places of Interest in the Neighbourhood
  A Picture in Brass (Hunsdon)
  Plotters Against Charles II (Stanstead Abbotts)
  A Poet's 'Fairy Palace' (Ware)

29 A Priory Out of Place

Position: Harpenden.
O.S. Map: Luton & Hertford area; Sheet 166; 1/50,000.
Map Ref: TL 136/132.
Access: Approaching the town from St Albans along the A1081, turn left down Redbourn Lane, walk along path on the right and the Priory is about 100 yards on the left.

Flowton Priory, a Tudor house, can claim to have a literally more moving history than any other building hereabouts. Originally, it was a priory house more than 70 miles away in Ipswich, and in 1928 it was dismantled, brick by brick, each brick being numbered to ease reassembly in Harpenden.

The date of the priory house is put at 1525. It has stained-glass windows (many decorated with coats of arms), timbered exterior walls and Tudor chimneys. Although the house is private and not open to the public, it is an impressive sight seen from the gate at the end of the drive.

Places of Interest in the Neighbourhood
  That Wicked Lady (Wheathampstead)
  Where Old Battles Were Fought (Wheathampstead)

The 'much-travelled' Flowton Priory

30 Bill Sikes's Quick One

Position: Old Hatfield village.
O.S. Map: Luton & Hertford area; Sheet 166; 1/50,000.
Map Ref: TL 235/086.
Access: The Eight Bells is on the corner of Fore St and Park St.

The Eight Bells is identified with the small public house mentioned in
Charles Dickens's *Oliver Twist* – where Bill Sikes and his dog briefly
found refuge after he had murdered Nancy. It was in the tap room that
Sikes encountered an 'antic fellow', half pedlar, half mountebank, who
was selling an 'infallible and invaluable composition for removing all
sorts of stain'.

The pedlar offered in all innocence to remove the bloodstain
(Nancy's blood) that he noticed on Bill Sikes's hat. But it was all too
near the knuckle for the villainous Sikes, who fearfully snatched up his
hat from the man and dashed out of the inn.

Dickens was no stranger to Hatfield. He visited it many times – on
one occasion when he was a reporter for *The Morning Chronicle*,
covering a big fire at Hatfield House. He also mentioned Hatfield in
later stories. 'Mrs Lirriper's Lodgings', from *Christmas Stories*, is told

Sikes's sanctuary: the Eight Bells, Hatfield

in the first-person by a finely drawn character, Mrs Lirriper, a widow
who ran a lodging house in Norfolk Street, Strand. She and her
husband spent their wedding day at the 'Salisbury Arms', a coaching
inn, now demolished, at the top of Fore Street, Hatfield, where Dickens
himself had stayed. Dickens had Mrs Lirriper's husband 'buried' in St
Etheldreda's churchyard nearby.

Places of Interest in the Neighbourhood
  A Garden from the Past (Hatfield)
  Burial Place of Three 'Prime Ministers' (Hatfield)
  Roman Bath Under the A1 (Welwyn)

The Marchioness of Salisbury's Tudor-style garden at Hatfield House

31 A Garden from the Past

Position: Hatfield House, Hatfield.
O.S. Map: Luton & Hertford area; Sheet 166; 1/50,000.
Map Ref: TL 237/084.
Access: Through the main gates from the A1000. Hatfield station (BR) is practically opposite. The House is two miles from the A1(M).

Outside the Old Palace at Hatfield House is one of several beautiful gardens created in the 1980s by the present Marchioness of Salisbury: a Tudor-style knot garden, reminiscent of the time when the young Princess Elizabeth lived in seclusion in the Palace before she became queen in 1558. (She was kept out of the way here as her Protestant sympathies had put her under the suspicion of her Catholic half-sister Mary).

A knot is a feature of an ornamental garden, set in a square. There are three such gardens here, each with an intricate design of interwoven ribbons (or knots) fashioned, in this instance, of low box hedges. Contained by them are bulbs and plants known to have been grown by John Tradescant, who was gardener (and a plant collector) with his son at Hatfield. Tradescant senior was gardener to both Robert Cecil – builder of Hatfield House – and his son for five years from 1610.

Accompanying the three knots, which give a display of 15th-, 16th- and 17th-century plants, is a foot maze, or labyrinth. This has been a feature of gardens from the earliest times. It was often planted as an allegory or symbol of the perplexities and intricacies which beset the Christian's path: Christian symbols of life's crises, from birth to death. It was made not to get lost in but for contemplation.

The whole pleasing pattern of the gardens, which are open to the public between the last week in March to the second Sunday in October, can be appreciated particularly when seen from the raised walks.

Hatfield House itself is Jacobean, but built in the Elizabethan style (its plan is the letter 'E', for Elizabeth), and completed in 1612. Apart from the magnificence of the building, it contains many treasures, including what have been claimed (though not proved) to be Elizabeth's hat, gloves and stockings, some fine portraits of her as queen, and a contemporary pedigree, which traces her ancestry back to Adam.

Places of Interest in the Neighbourhood
  Bill Sikes's Quick One (Hatfield)
  Burial Place of Three 'Prime Ministers' (Hatfield)
  Roman Bath Under the A1 (Welwyn)

32   Burial Place of Three 'Prime Ministers'

Position: Old Hatfield.
O.S. Map: Luton & Hertford area; Sheet 166; 1/50,000.
Map Ref: TL 235/085.
Access: St Etheldreda's Church, which is two miles from the A1(M), is at the top of Fore Street hill. Hatfield station (BR) is a few hundred yards away.

When the diarist Samuel Pepys visited Hatfield Parish Church – St Etheldreda's – in Old Hatfield in the 1660s, he 'did hear a most excellent good sermon which pleased me mightily and very devout', and he noted that he saw Lord Salisbury there.

Few churches are so overlaid with history as this one, being closely linked with one of England's most influential families, the Cecils.

Two great officers of state are buried here, and another in the Salisburys' private burial ground close by the church. In the Salisbury Chapel is an impressive white marble tomb, in which lies Robert Cecil, the first Earl, who became Secretary of State (equivalent to Prime Minister) to Queen Elizabeth I, and Lord High Treasurer to James I.

The tomb of Robert Cecil in St Etheldreda's Church, Old Hatfield

He died in 1612. The Earl's effigy, in Garter robes, on a black marble slab, is supported by the four kneeling figures of Prudence, Justice, Fortitude and Temperance. Below it lies a skeleton, symbolising mortality.

Also commemorated in the church is the 2nd Viscount Melbourne, who served as Prime Minister under William IV, and then Queen Victoria, to whom he was guide and mentor in the early years of her reign. He died in 1848. His burial place, south-west of the chancel, is indicated merely by a plaque on a pillar near the pulpit – the entrance to the vault is nearby.

The remains of the great Victorian Prime Minister, the 3rd Marquess – Robert Gascoyne-Cecil (1830-1903) – are not in the church but in the adjacent family burial ground a little way to the east of it. But there is a cenotaph in the Salisbury Chapel in the church (and one of similar design in Westminster Abbey). The Marquess was three times Prime Minister in Queen Victoria's reign, at a time when the British Empire was at its most expansive and influential.

Places of Interest in the Neighbourhood
  A Garden from the Past (Hatfield)
  Bill Sikes's Quick One (Hatfield)
  Roman Bath Under the A1 (Welwyn)

33 Fox's Ancient Chair

Position: Hertford.
O.S. Map: Luton & Hertford area; Sheet 166; 1/50,000.
Map Ref: TL 328/128.
Access: The Friends Meeting House is in Railway Street.

The carved oak chair in the entrance hall of the Friends Meeting House, in Hertford, is a venerable reminder of Quakerism's historic struggles and of their founder, George Fox, who is traditionally believed to have sat in it during his attendances there. It is known, in fact, as Fox's Chair.

This is the oldest surviving purpose-built Meeting House in the world that is still in use: the date of its building, 1670, is engraved above the outside door. The furnishing is rather spartan, with the original wooden high-backed seating (now, unlike formerly, with cushions) still in situ. Along the back of the hall are the original wooden clothes pegs, and there is also a four-tier platform – the Ministers' Stand – formerly used by ministers, elders and overseers – which is unique.

Hertford Quakers still meet regularly on Sundays in this wonderfully atmospheric building, which they are happy to show visitors round.

From the late 1650s onwards the Quakers suffered painfully in the cause of freedom to worship in the way they wanted. There were five prisoners of conscience in Hertford Gaol in 1658, out of 124 all over the country.

But the Restoration of the monarchy brought even worse persecution: the Quaker Act of 1662 and the revival of older legislation led not only to more imprisonments but forfeiture of estate for, among other 'offences', attending Quaker meetings and refusing to attend parish churches. Among prisoners at Hertford were Henry Stout (reputed to have invented the drink, stout), Nicholas Lucas, a founder of Pennsylvania, and Henry Sweeting, a butcher, who contributed towards the cost of building this Meeting House.

Freedom of worship is taken for granted today in Britain, but not by the Quakers, who had to struggle for it for decades. Fox's Chair serves as a perpetual reminder of their determination and faith.

Places of Interest in the Neighbourhood
  Dr Dimsdale, Russian Baron (Bengeo)
  'Father' of the New River (Great Amwell)
  Kings of the Castle (Hertford)

34 Kings of the Castle

Position: Hertford.
O.S. Map: Luton & Hertford area; Sheet 166; 1/50,000.
Map Ref: TL 326/125.
Access: The Castle is a short walk from the town centre.

Few local government employees work amid the ambience of a
15th-century building, but that is the good fortune of many of those of
Hertford Town Council. The fine brick gateway, restored in about
1800, is the biggest visible remnant of Hertford Castle, near the town
centre, though there are stretches of flint walling (with an early
14th-century postern gate) and a mound, in the attractive gardens here
on the banks of the river Lea.

A granite obelisk near the main entrance to the castle announces:
'Near this spot was held the first General Synod of the English church
on September 24th, 673 AD, under the Presidency of Theodore of
Tarsus, 7th Archbishop of Canterbury and first Primate of All
England.' There were five bishops at the Synod: those of East Anglia,
Rochester, Wessex, Mercia and Northumbria.

In Norman times the castle was besieged by the King of France, and
Queen Isabella, mother of Edward III, lived and died here.

Places of Interest in the Neighbourhood
  Dr Dimsdale, Russian Baron (Bengeo)
  Fox's Ancient Chair (Hertford)
  A Poet's 'Fairy Palace' (Ware)

35 Steam Up to Stardom

Position: On the Hertford loop line (BR).
O.S. Map: Luton & Hertford area; Sheet 166; 1:50,000.
Access: From any station (BR) on the line from Wood Green to Stevenage, via Hertford.

The quiet little loopline that begins at Wood Green, enters Hertfordshire at Crews Hill and passes through countryside at Cuffley, Bayford and Hertford before rejoining the main line to the North at Stevenage, formed the setting of a 1929 half-sound, half-talkie film, 'The Flying Scotsman'.

The famous locomotive, of the Pacific 4-6-2 type that formed the basis of the impressive LNER streamliners, was a more familiar sight racing up the main line from King's Cross through Welwyn and Hitchin to Edinburgh, but in 1929 the 'Flying Scotsman' performed in the film's title role. Featuring in it was the Welsh-born film actor Ray Milland, long before he went to Hollywood to star in such films as 'Dial M for Murder' and the Oscar-winning 'Lost Weekend'. He died in 1986 at the age of 76.

Milland was picked for the role of footplate fireman because he could shovel coal convincingly: he had earlier been a South Wales miner. The driver in the film was played by Moore Marriott, later to star as the old man with Will Hay and Graham Moffatt in vintage film comedies such as 'Oh, Mr Porter'.

In 'The Flying Scotsman', which told the story of an attempt to wreck the train, two of the cast edged along the coaches' running boards towards the driving cab. This was no stunt: it was real enough. The trick was to shoot slowly and project normally to give the impression of high speed.

36 The Clutterbuck Connection

Position: Hinxworth, north of Ashwell.
O.S. Map: Bedford & Huntingdon area; Sheet 153; 1/50,000
Map Ref: TL 239/396.
Access: Although a private house and not open to view, Hinxworth Place can be seen by taking the public footpath from Ashwell Road (opp. Bury End Farm) to a road (right of way) leading to the house.

Hinxworth, Hertfordshire's northernmost village, has two curiosities, both linked by that noted county family, the Clutterbucks, many members of whom lived in Watford and Bushey.

Hinxworth Place dates from 1390, and was the home of two Lord Mayors of London as well as Robert Clutterbuck (1772-1831), one of the county's most distinguished historians, who bought it in 1801. Robert Clutterbuck is famous in the county for his monumental work *The History and Antiquities of the County of Hertford*, still to be seen in the county's public libraries. It took its author 18 years to write and compile, the first of the three volumes being published in 1815, the year of the Battle of Waterloo.

The war memorial at Hinxworth

Occupants of Hinxworth Place, a private residence, have included actors, artists and, the owner for many years now, a leading sculptor, John W. Mills.

Major A. Vincent Clutterbuck, a descendant of Robert, provided the second curiosity in Hinxworth. This is an unusual clocktower war memorial which stands at the roadside (junction of High St and New Inn Rd; map ref TL 236/405). It was obviously well-intentioned, but with its blue dials and cream-washed rendering, it seems to be rather out of keeping with the locality.

The clock commemorates local people who died in the first World War – including Major Clutterbuck himself. The memorial is inscribed with the names of 12 local dead of World War I, and one of World War II.

Places of Interest in the Neighbourhood
    Lament of the Black Death (Ashwell)
    Pepys Deciphered (Baldock)
    The Enigma of the Cave (Royston)

Memorial to the air crash victims, near Hitchin

37 The Tragedy of Two Air Pioneers

Position: Near Willian, Hitchin.
O.S. Map: Luton & Hertford area; Sheet 166; 1/50,000.
Map Ref: TL 220/299.
Access: The obelisk stands on the east side of the road between Willian
and Great Wymondley, a mile east of Hitchin.

How many people, I wonder, pause at this roadside memorial, puzzled
at its teasingly uninformative inscription: 'In memory of Captain
Hamilton and Lt Wyness-Stuart, who lost their lives whilst serving their
country as aviators, Sept 6th, 1912'.

This stone commemorates one of the earliest air crashes in Britain, in
which two 30-year-old officers in the newly-formed Royal Flying
Corps, the forerunner of the RAF, were killed. The pilot, Capt. Patrick
Hamilton, was the first English officer to meet his death while actually
flying under orders on His Majesty's Service. Hitchin and its
surrounding villages were deeply moved by the tragedy.

The crash, near this spot, occurred during reconnaissance in
connection with local military manoeuvres. Capt. Hamilton, an
experienced pilot, was at the controls of a 100 h.p. Deperdussin
monoplane, with Lt Wyness-Stuart as observer. The aircraft had made
an early-morning take-off from Farnborough, and while passing over
Graveley, near Hitchin, suddenly spiralled downwards. At a height of
about 400 feet a wing was seen to crumple up, and the plane hit the
ground out of control. The cause of the crash was apparently a fault in
an engine valve. A loose cowl damaged the wing-strut wires, which
became entangled with the rotary engine.

One of the witnesses at the inquest was Walter Brett, landlord of the
George & Dragon public house at Graveley, who saw the plane come
down at the end of his meadow at about seven in the morning.

When the funeral took place in St Saviour's Church, Radcliffe Road,
Hitchin, the approach roads were thronged with members of the public,
but sadly the church was so crowded with Service personnel that none
could get in. The memorial on the Willian-Great Wymondley road,
paid for by public subscription, was their way of paying tribute. Capt.
Hamilton was buried in Hythe, Sussex, and Lt Stuart in Mells,
Somerset.

Places of Interest in the Neighbourhood
  Sir Ebenezer's Dream (Letchworth)
  Church of the Horse (St Ippollitts)

38 The Samaritan Woman

Position: Hoddesdon.
O.S. Map: Luton & Hertford area; Sheet 166; 1/50,000.
Map Ref: TL 372/082.
Access: The figure stands in the garden beside Lowewood Museum, in the High Street.

The stone figure here, known as the 'Samaritan Woman', represents an important stage in the town's history.

For years, Hoddesdon had to rely for its water on private wells. In around 1622, when Mr (later Sir) Marmaduke Rawdon came to live in Hoddesdon, he provided himself with a supply of piped water from a point near High Grounds (now called High Leigh) in Lord Street, about half a mile west of Hoddesdon.

A few years later, apparently finding that he had more water than he needed, he laid another pipe to the south end of the Market Place, marking the spot with the figure of the Samaritan Woman. The water from the pipe fed through the urn she was (and is) holding, and this flowed into a pond, from which Hoddesdon's citizens could collect it.

The statue was moved, and the pond filled in, in 1826. Eventually, a more efficient piped water system came into use and the figure was moved several times before coming to rest outside the Lowewood Museum in Hoddesdon. Its name was derived from the Biblical story of the Woman of Samaria whom Christ met at Jacob's Well, but the identity of the sculptor is uncertain. Edmund Parlett, Vicar of Broxbourne, who was a poet, is believed to have written verses which express the town's gratitude to the provider of its first water supply:

> A nymph of stone, who from an urn doth pour
> Into the pitchers of both rich and poor,
> Her limpid treasures from the Western Vale.
> Whose unexhausted bounties seldom fail,
> And never grudging, ever generous she,
> With the first element for making tea.
> Thanks generous Rawdon for thy kind bequest,
> Remotest ages shall the donor bless.

Places of Interest in the Neighbourhood
  Wren's Banished Gateway (Cheshunt)
  The King and the Tinker (Cheshunt)
  Plotters Against Charles II (Stanstead Abbotts)

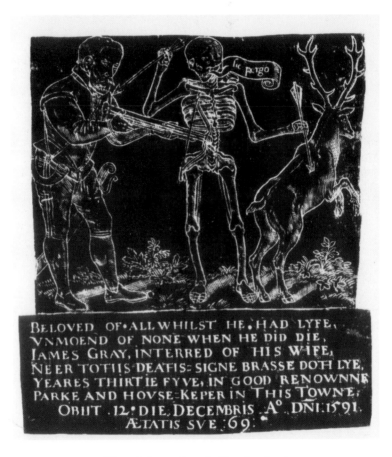

The inscription reads:

BELOVED OF•ALL WHILST HE•HAD LYFE,
VNMOEND OF NONE WHEN HE DID DIE,
IAMES GRAY, INTERRED OF HIS WIFE,
NE ER TOTIIS DEATIS: SIGNE BRASSE DOTH LYE,
YEARES THIRTIE FYVE, IN GOOD RENOWNNE
PARKE AND HOVSE-KEPER IN THIS TOWNE,
OBIIT 12: DIE DECEMBRIS A° DNI 1591.
ÆTATIS SVE 69.

The park-keeper brass in Hunsdon church

39 Memorial to a Park-keeper

Position: Hunsdon, north-east of Stanstead Abbotts.
O.S. Map: Chelmsford & Harlow area; Sheet 167; 1/50,000.
Map Ref: TL 418/127.
Access: Take the A414 eastwards from Harlow; church is on the right about a mile up road to Hunsdon.

Hunsdon's rebuilt 15th-century church, dedicated to St Dunstan, Archbishop of Canterbury in 961 AD, contains one of the most pictorially interesting of Hertfordshire's figure brasses.

Fixed in the church's north wall is the memorial to a popular local character, James Gray, who was killed – while out hunting it is thought – in 1591.

The plate is 53cm x 48cm (21in x 19in) and shows a skeleton, representing Death, jabbing both Gray and a stag with arrows. The skeleton is saying, in Latin, 'Sic pergo', which has been variously translated as 'So I proceed', 'Thus I go on till the same fate befalls me' and 'I do as you do'.

The engraving is fairly rudimentary and anatomically inaccurate, but the stag is beautifully drawn, and in perspective.

The inscription reads:

> Beloved of all whilst he had Lyfe
> Unmoaned of none when he did die
> JAMES GRAY interred of his Wyfe
> Near to this Death's Signe Brass doth lye;
> Years thirty-five in good renown
> Parke and Housekeeper of this Town.

The church was built about half a mile from the village proper, for the convenience originally of those who lived in the adjacent Hunsdon House. Both buildings were erected at roughly the same period. The original mid-15th-century building was rebuilt by Henry VIII in about 1525, and was occupied in their youth by two children who were to become queens of England: Elizabeth and Mary.

Places of Interest in the Neighbourhood
  'Father' of the New River (Great Amwell)
  Man and Nature in Bronze (Perry Green)
  Plotters Against Charles II (Stanstead Abbotts)

40   Buried in the 'Wrong' Tomb?

Position: Kings Langley, south of Hemel Hempstead.
O.S. Map: Luton & Hertford area; Sheet 166; 1/50,000.
Map Ref: TL 073/025.
Access: The church is in Church Lane, just off the High Street.

In the parish church of All Saints, Kings Langley, occupying a special
chapel set aside for it, is a mysterious tomb which – it is claimed – has
never contained the royal personage it was intended for. At present it
contains three bodies. One is that of Edmund of Langley – first Duke of
York, a son of Edward III and a younger brother of the Black Prince –
who lived in a royal palace west of the High Street and died in 1402.
The second is that of his wife Isabel of Castile. The third is of an
unknown woman, discovered when the tomb was opened in 1878.

   The tomb, of alabaster and Purbeck marble, was once in the Friary
Church at Langley, but was removed to the parish church of All Saints
in around 1557, where it stood in the chancel, as the fine old engraving
shows. In 1877 it was moved to the Memorial Chapel, and Queen
Victoria presented a glorious stained-glass window, which repeats the
coats-of-arms appearing along one side and both ends of the tomb.

   Then who should be in the tomb? This question intrigued Mr Enoch
Powell, MP, in 1965. 'I happened, when passing through on the A5, to
look in to see the tomb attributed to the Duke of York, and my
suspicions were at once aroused,' he told me. And he became
convinced, after studying the coats-of-arms adorning it that the tomb
was not intended for Edmund of Langley or Isabel, but for someone
else.

   In an article in the magazine *History Today* in 1965 he wrote: 'There
is only one person for whom a tomb could have been made which bore
at its head the undifferenced arms of England, flanked by the two royal
saints. That person is a king of England. There is only one king of
England on whose tomb these particular arms could be placed. That
king is Richard II.'

   Mr Powell argues that the tomb was originally not intended for
Edmund at all. It had been ordered for Richard II for himself and his
wife Anne of Bohemia. But this plan was frustrated when Anne
predeceased him in 1394. So Richard placed it at the disposal of
Edmund.

   Richard II came to an unhappy end. Although his father was the
Black Prince, unlike his father he was a weakling, physically and
morally, who had difficulty in maintaining power. He was deposed by

Edmund of Langley's tomb - a Victorian engraving

Henry Bolingbroke, and spent the last part of his life in prison in Pontefract, Yorkshire, where he died mysteriously.

His body was brought south, and last rites were performed in the old St Paul's Cathedral in London. By Henry IV's command, it was conveyed the same night to the Friary at Kings Langley, where it was buried privately at dawn. But not in the tomb.

Fourteen years later, as an act of expiation, Henry V had Richard's body exhumed and buried with great pomp in Westminster Abbey in a marble tomb with gilded effigies. It stands there today, next to Edward the Confessor's.

Places of Interest in the Neighbourhood
    Birthplace of England's Only Pope (Abbots Langley)
    The Plague Door (Sarratt)
    Charlie Chaplin Played Here (Watford)

41 Sir Edward's Stately Fantasy

Position: Old Knebworth.
O.S. Map: Luton & Hertford area; Sheet 166; 1/50,000.
Map Ref: TL 230/208.
Access: Knebworth House is about a mile east of the A1(M). Turn off at junction 7, and follow signs.

Knebworth House is the strangest-looking of stately homes, and certainly one of the most interesting. A distinguished literary scion of a distinguished family, the famous novelist Sir Edward Bulwer-Lytton, was responsible for this. No sooner had he inherited the house in 1843 than he engaged an architect to carry out the bizarre additions. He saw the house as a gothic palace rather than a large mansion, and added the amazing array of gothic ornamentation - turrets, cupolas, towers, gargoyles, griffins and dragons – that adorn its roof. All combine to give it an intriguing air of fantasy.

The ornate roof of Knebworth House

The first member of the family to own a house on this site – in 1492 – was Sir Robert Lytton, a favourite of Henry VII, with whom he fought at Bosworth. Much of the work on the present house and garden is the work of Sir Edwin Lutyens – brother-in-law of the second Earl. Today the house is packed with portraits, beautiful furniture and historic artefacts collected over the centuries. These include a crucifix given by Mary Queen of Scots to one of her ladies-in-waiting before her execution, and a ring which Charles I gave to a friend before his death.

Another notable Victorian member of the Lytton family was Sir Robert, the lst Earl, who became Viceroy of India. He organised the Delhi Durbar of 1877 at which Queen Victoria was declared Empress of India. A permanent exhibition at Knebworth, the Raj Collection, recalls the great days of the British Empire with items such as the Viceroy's banner for the durbar, as well as the Earl's robes.

When the 2nd Earl died in 1947, Knebworth House passed to his daughter, Lady Hermione Bulwer-Lytton. She married Cameron Cobbold, who became Governor of the Bank of England, Lord Chamberlain and then Baron Cobbold of Knebworth. The house, now occupied by the 2nd Lord Cobbold and his family, is open (together with the gardens) to the public from April to September.

Places of Interest in the Neighbourhood
   Meeting Place of Kings (Benington)
   A Right Royal Error (St Paul's Walden)
   Dick Turpin's Getaway (Stevenage)

42 Lemsford's Water Music

Position: Lemsford, north of Hatfield.
O.S. Map: Luton & Hertford area; Sheet 166; 1/50.000.
Map Ref: TL 220/124.
Access: The old mill is a few hundred yards from the B197, off the Al(M), two miles north of Hatfield.

If there's a song one's heard a thousand times raising the roof in the more boisterous public houses, it's 'Nellie Dean'. For the inspiration for that, the Victorian composer J. P. Skelly has to thank Lemsford village. The old mill by the stream – the river Lea – is still there.

Tradition has it that when Skelly was staying at nearby Brocket Hall (see 'Scandal of Lady Caroline') he went out for a stroll and was charmed by Lemsford village. His inspiration to write the song was sparked by the sight of a pretty girl on the bridge across the river:

> There's an old mill by the stream, Nellie Dean,
> Where we used to sit and dream, Nellie Dean.
> And the waters as they flow
> Seem to murmur soft and low,
> You're my heart's desire,
> I love you, Nellie Dean.

Places of Interest in the Neighbourhood
  Bernard Shaw's 'Dell and Dwelling' (Ayot St Lawrence)
  Divided in Death (Ayot St Lawrence)
  Scandal of Lady Caroline (Lemsford)

*Song-writer's inspiration: the old mill
by the stream, Lemsford*

43 Scandal of Lady Caroline

Position: Near Wheathampstead.
O.S. Map: Luton & Hertford area; Sheet 166; 1/50,000.
Map Ref: TL 212/131.
Access: Brocket Hall is not open to the public, but it can be seen in the distance from Marford Road between Lemsford and Wheathampstead (B653). There is a closer view of it to be had from the bridge in Brocket Park, reached by taking (and keeping to) the public footpath from opposite the Crooked Chimney in Marford Road.

Brocket Hall, the 18th-century home of the great Hertfordshire family, the Brockets, has had a noteworthy history. Not only did two Victorian Prime Ministers, Lords Melbourne and Palmerston, die there, but it was the setting for a famous scandal involving Lord Melbourne's wife, the beautiful, witty, histrionic Lady Caroline Lamb, gifted as a poet and novelist and lover of many members of the literati.

Lady Caroline's behaviour was a great trial to Melbourne, who suffered her various amours with only the mildest admonishment. What Lady Caroline really wanted was attention; hence the flirtations that were to be her downfall.

She fancied herself as an author, and wrote a novel of which Lord Byron was the hero. She yearned to meet Byron, whose 'Childe Harold' impressed her deeply.

Their liaison began at a party. Lady Caroline became infatuated with him, and their relationship became the talk of London society. But because Byron himself flirted in public, Lady Caroline frequently

Brocket Hall, former home of the scandalous Lady Caroline Lamb

became jealous. In 1813 Byron grew bored with her and they quarrelled. Finally, she persuaded some local girls to dress in white and sing while dancing round a fire, on which she threw Byron's letters.

One day in 1824, as she was leaving Brocket Park, Lady Caroline saw a funeral procession passing by. When she inquired whose it was, she was told it was Byron's. The poet's body had been brought from Greece, where he had died of a fever, and was being conveyed to his native village, Hucknall Torkard, in Nottinghamshire.

Lady Caroline was so shocked that she became seriously mentally deranged, and died four years later. It was only after her death that her husband, Lord Melbourne, till then preoccupied with his wife's behaviour, was able to make headway in politics. He became Prime Minister briefly in 1834, then again from 1835 to 1841, becoming guide and mentor to the young Queen Victoria in the early years of her reign. Melbourne died at Brocket Hall in 1848.

The house is still the Brocket family home and is also is a residential conference centre.

Places of Interest in the Neighbourhood
  Bernard Shaw's 'Dell and Dwelling' (Ayot St Lawrence)
  Divided in Death (Ayot St Lawrence)
  Lemsford's Water Music (Lemsford)

Sir Ebenezer Howard's shorthand typewriter and desk, Letchworth

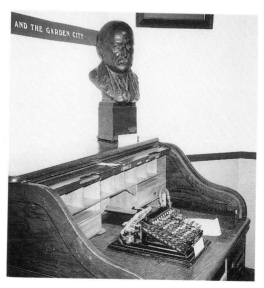

44 Sir Ebenezer's Dream

Position: Letchworth.
O.S. Map: Luton & Hertford area; Sheet 166; 1/50,000.
Map Ref: TL 222/324.
Access: The First Garden City Heritage Museum is at No 296 Norton Way South, near the junction with Pixmore Way.

The bustling town of Letchworth, England's first garden city, is a living testimony to the imagination of one man: Sir Ebenezer Howard, who fathered not just one, but four other new towns in Hertfordshire: Welwyn Garden City, built in 1920, followed by Stevenage, Hemel Hempstead and Hatfield.

  Sir Ebenezer, who was born in London in 1850, spent much of his professional life as a Parliamentary shorthand writer. In fact, one of his inventions was the prototype of a shorthand typewriter, which is displayed on his desk (along with a plaster bust by Ivy Young) in the First Garden City Heritage Museum. It never went into production.

  When shorthand writer to the Royal Commission on Labour in the 1880s, Sir Ebenezer noted how dissatisfaction with workers' living conditions was expressed by everyone at all levels. It was this, and his acquaintance with Keir Hardie, Tom Mann and John Burns, that fired his determination to create a garden city.

  In 1898 he outlined his concept in 'Tomorrow: a Peaceful Path to Real Reform', published as *Garden Cities of Tomorrow* four years later. It visualised garden cities each with population limited to 32,000 and surrounded by agricultural land. Six of these would be clustered around a central city (pop 58,000) with radial railway links to the satellites. The new towns would be self-contained units, where people would work as well as live. The social and the architectural, open spaces, people and industry... all would be in harmony. And so it has largely turned out.

  Sir Ebenezer died in Welwyn Garden City in 1928, and is buried in Letchworth Garden City Cemetery.

Places of Interest in the Neighbourhood
  Pepys Deciphered (Baldock)
  The Tragedy of Two Air Pioneers (Hitchin)
  Miss Lawrence's 'Folly' (Letchworth)

45 Miss Lawrence's 'Folly'

Position: Letchworth.
O.S. Map: Luton & Hertford area; Sheet 166; 1/50,000.
Map Ref: TL 221/315.
Access: The Cloisters faces the junction of Cloisters Road and
Barrington Road.

The Cloisters is certainly one of the most hotch-potch buildings in the
county, but it is not really a folly. In having it built when she settled in
Letchworth in 1906, the eccentric Miss Annie Jane Lawrence intended
it to promote her belief that fresh air nourished both the body and
mind. She called her philosophy the Open Air Life, and it was at The
Cloisters that its devotees gathered.

 The building lacks any architectural unity, and is a chaotic mixture of
flint and brick in various colours, towers and turrets and dozens of
vertical rectangular windows. Almost every feature is adorned with
some kind of symbol: even the lead rainwater heads and drainpipes
depict birds, and other small creatures, such as bats and moths.

 In later years, the strange house developed a substantial musical
tradition, and became a lively centre for crafts. In 1948, Miss Lawrence
(who died in 1953) offered The Cloisters for the use of the Freemasons
of Letchworth – an offer that was gratefully accepted. It has been their
'home' ever since.

Places of Interest in the Neighbourhood
 Pepys Deciphered (Baldock)
 The Tragedy of Two Air Pioneers (Hitchin)
 Sir Ebenezer's Dream (Letchworth)

46 In Memory of Bishop Ken

Position: Little Berkhamsted, east of Hatfield.
O.S. Map: Luton & Hertford; Sheet 166; 1/50,000.
Map Ref: TL 292/079.
Access: The church is Church Road, at the junction with Robin's Nest Hill.

Thomas Ken, a noted cleric in his day, was born in Little Berkhamsted in 1637 and has been a source of some pride among the village church congregation ever since. Nearly a century ago a new altar was provided, bearing a carved mitre with the initials T.K. – Thomas Ken – at one end.

Though small of stature, Bishop Ken had a wide-ranging, scholarly mind. He was the author of several hymns, including 'Awake my soul, and with the sun...' and 'Glory to Thee, my God, this night...', both of which are still sung in churches throughout the land.

Ken, who attended Winchester, wrote many learned works, books and poetry, and was a close friend of Izaak Walton, author of *The Compleat Angler*. Ken was appointed chaplain to King Charles II, of whom he was highly critical over his immoral lifestyle, and was incensed when asked to provide lodging for Nell Gwynn on her visit to Winchester. 'A woman of ill-repute ought not to be endured in the house of a clergyman, least of all the King's Chaplain,' he said.

Not only was the king unrepenting, but also forgiving. 'Little Ken tells me my faults,' he said. And, later, Ken was made Bishop of Bath & Wells - by the very monarch he criticised. He became bishop in 1685, spent five turbulent years through the Monmouth Rebellion and the reigns of James II and William of Orange, who deprived him of his See. Bishop Ken then retired to oblivion at Longleat, where he lived on a small pension from Viscount Weymouth, and died in 1711.

Places of Interest in the Neighbourhood
  The Frightened Rector (Essendon)
  Fox's Ancient Chair (Hertford)
  The Watchtower that Wasn't (Little Berkhamsted)

47 The Watchtower that Wasn't

Position: Little Berkhamsted, south-west of Hertford.
O.S. Map: Luton & Hertford area; Sheet 166; 1/50,000.
Map Ref: TL 295/082.
Access: Stratton's Folly stands towards the top of Robin's Nest Hill,
one mile south of the B158.

This tall, handsome 100ft red brick tower, known as Stratton's Folly,
was a folly indeed. It was built in 1789 as an observatory, and in order
that its owner, John Stratton, a retired admiral, could stand on the
battlements and see ships plying up and down the Thames – in fact, a
practical impossibility.

The Admiral destroyed all documents relating to the building,
because he did not want his heirs to know how much it cost to build.
The octagonal five-storey Folly, which has rooms 18ft in diameter, is
now listed as being of special architectural and historic interest.

In the 1960s its then owner, Mr William Tatton-Brown, an architect,
having rescued it from disrepair, sought planning permission to convert
it into residential accommodation. A public inquiry was held, and there
were objections from neighbours who complained that they would be
overlooked, among them an MP who lived nearby and said that
because he sunbathed in the nude it would be an invasion of his privacy.

Stratton's Folly is still privately owned and occupied.

Places of Interest in the Neighbourhood
   The Frightened Rector (Essendon)
   Fox's Ancient Chair (Hertford)
   In Memory of Bishop Ken (Little Berkhamsted)

48 The Canal Duke

Position: On the Ashridge Estate. west Herts.
O.S. Map: Aylesbury & Leighton Buzzard area; Sheet 165;
    1/50,000.
Map Ref: SP 970/131.
Access: For the Bridgewater monument, take the A41(T) and turn off
on the B4506 west of Berkhamsted; then drive about half a mile
westwards through the estate to the monument.

The Bridgewater Monument is an imposing granite Doric column
surmounted by an urn, which towers over the 4,000-acre Ashridge

Estate (National Trust). It was erected in 1832 to commemorate the 'Canal Duke', the eccentric third Duke of Bridgewater, whose niche in history was secured by building 10 miles of canal across an aqueduct between his coal-mine at Worsley, and Manchester, thus becoming the founder of inland navigation in Britain.

The monument is open to the public and offers fine views of the surrounding countryside. The idyllic woodland, park and gardens in which it stands were landscaped by Capability Brown in 1760 and Repton in the early 19th century, and are open to the public, though not, except on rare occasions, Ashridge House itself, which serves as a management college and whose neo-Gothic tower, turrets, spire and archway can easily be seen from the grounds.

Places of Interest in the Neighbourhood
Where the Saxons Surrendered (Berkhamsted)
The Silent Zoo (Tring)

The first Mosquito: the prototype at London Colney

49 The 'Wooden Wonder'

Position: London Colney, south-east of St Albans.
O.S. Map: Luton & Hertford area; Sheet 166; 1:50,000.
Map Ref: TL 195/028.
Access: The drive into the Mosquito Museum is off the A111, about half a mile from London Colney village.

The Mosquito Museum is not some kind of entomological exhibition, as a friend of mine thought, but an unusual aircraft museum, housed in hangars next to the moated 17th-century manor house of Salisbury Hall. It features a number of De Havilland aircraft, but the star of the show is the prototype, painted in smart yellow livery, of that famous plane of World War II, the De Havilland Mosquito.

This versatile twin-engined bomber, made almost entirely of wood, was a revolutionary concept for its time; hence its sobriquet, the 'Wooden Wonder'. It was designed and developed here at the Hall in 1940 and manufactured some miles away at Hatfield. More than 7,700 Mosquitoes were produced. Their wartime duties included photo-reconnaissance, mine-laying, torpedo dropping, as a day and night fighter, and submarine killer. They were capable of carrying a 4,000lb 'blockbuster' bomb.

Perhaps the Mosquito's most memorable role was in the Pathfinder Force of Air Vice Marshal Donald Bennett, which illuminated targets for Allied bomber forces over Germany.

On the way to the museum, visitors can see, through an arch, Salisbury Hall itself (closed to the public). In a house on this site lived the Earl of Warwick (the Kingmaker), and Nell Gwynne lived in a cottage which is still there, next to the moat.

Here, it is said, Nell successfully persuaded a reluctant Charles II to give a title to one of their three illegitimate children. Suddenly rushing to the window, she held the child over a 30ft drop into the moat until the horrified king shouted: 'Spare the Duke of St Albans!' – the name of the nearby city being the first that sprang to mind.

Winston Churchill stayed at Salisbury Hall with his mother, Lady Randolph Churchill, when she lived here in 1905. Until De Havillands took it over during World War II, Salisbury Hall was the home of Sir Nigel Gresley, the LNER locomotive designer. It is still privately owned.

Places of Interest in the Neighbourhood
  Roses, Roses All the Way (Chiswell Green)
  A War Leader's Last Resting-place (Ridge)

50 Essayist's Holiday Home

Position: Mackerye End, north-east of Harpenden.
O.S. Map: Luton & Hertford area; Sheet 166; 1/50,000.
Map Ref: TL 156/156.
Access: To reach Mackerye End, turn up minor road at Batford, east of Harpenden. Old rear of Mackery End Farm house can be seen, with permission, from the farmyard, but visited inside only by special arrangement.

Unlike Button Snap (see 'Lamb's Legacy'), Charles Lamb frequently stayed at Mackery End Farm in his childhood. The front of the house is of later date, but the old part, as known by Lamb, is at the rear.

In an essay on Mackery End, Lamb wrote with affection and nostalgia about the farm:

'The oldest thing I remember is Mackery End; or Mackarel End, as it is spelt, in some old maps of Hertfordshire; a farmhouse – delightfully situated within a gentle walk from Wheathampstead. I can just remember having been there, on a visit to a great-aunt, when I was a child, under the care of Bridget [His sister Mary].... The sight of the old farmhouse, though every trace of it was effaced from my recollection, affected me with a pleasure which I had not experienced for many a year....'

He first visited Mackery End in around 1779. One of the attractions of Hertfordshire for Lamb was that a number of his ancestors lived there.

Places of Interest in the Neighbourhood
   A Priory Out of Place (Harpenden)
   That Wicked Lady (Wheathampstead)
   Where Old Battles Were Fought (Wheathampstead)

51 An Ancient Beacon

Position: Monken Hadley, near Barnet.
O.S. Map: Luton & Hertford area; Sheet 166; 1/50,000.
Map Ref: TQ 250/975.
Access: Turn down Dury Road, off the Gt North Road, north of
Barnet; Monken Hadley church is on the left.

The cresset beacon adorning the flint and ironstone tower of Monken
Hadley Parish Church is a great rarity, according to Pevsner. It has
been lit in celebration of national events for the past 500 years. The date
above the west door is 1494, so the claim that it helped to blaze out a
warning of the approach of the Spanish Armada in 1588 is certainly
feasible. It was later lit to announce the Jacobite risings of 1715 and
1745. In 1988 it was one of a chain of beacons nationwide lit to mark
the 400th anniversary of the Armada.

The beacon's 'bucket' is about 70 feet above street level, on what was
known in the time of the first Queen Elizabeth as Beacon Hill. Hadley
village is about 425 feet above sea level and is in a generally
commanding position. Barnet is the highest point on the original Great
North Road between London and York – an ideal site for a beacon.

Places of Interest in the Neighbourhood
   Where Warwick the Kingmaker Died (Barnet)
   Night of the Zeppelin (Cuffley)
   A War Leader's Last Resting-place (Ridge)

52   Gateway to Nowhere

Position: North Mymms.
O.S. Map: Luton & Hertford area; Sheet 166; 1:50,000.
Map Ref: TL 254/050.
Access: Folly Arch stands in Hawkshead Road (off A1000) a mile or so north of Potters Bar.

Folly Arch, a well-known local landmark, is a mock-medieval remnant of the estate of Gobions, where once stood the house of 'Gubbins'. The arch was originally intended to be seen from the distance as a romantic ruin, though at one time it may have been an entrance to the estate.

More Hall, a house on this estate, was once owned by the More family, whose most famous member, Sir Thomas, became Speaker of the House of Commons, and Chancellor of England, under Henry VIII. Being loyal to the Pope, Sir Thomas felt unable to recognise the annulment of the king's marriage to Catharine of Aragon and refused too to recognise Henry as head of the Church of England in place of the Pope. So he was condemned to death and executed.

Today he is commemorated in the name of Chancellor's School in Brookmans Park.

The house 'Gubbins' was pulled down by the owner of another estate, Brookmans, who added the land to his property.

The 18th-century Folly Arch was built by Sir Jeremy Sambrooke, who also erected the Battle of Barnet memorial at Hadley (See 'Where Warwick the Kingmaker Died') when owner of Gobions. At one time a path from it led down through an avenue of trees to pleasure gardens, where the attractions included a lake, woodland temple and bowling green. Gobions is now a public open space, but only the lake remains.

The original way through Folly Arch is now impassable. Access is from Mymms Drive or Moffats Lane.

Is there any truth in the story that a farthing was placed under each brick during construction? Who knows?

Places of Interest in the Neighbourhood
   Home of Miss Muffet? (Brookmans Park)
   'Customs' Posts for Coal (Brookmans Park)
   A War Leader's Last Resting-place (Ridge)

Folly Arch, North Mymms

53 Man and Nature in Bronze

Position: Perry Green, south-west of Bishop's Stortford.
O.S. Map: Chelmsford & Harlow area; Sheet 167; 1/50,000.
Map Ref: TL 438/175.
Access: Dane Tree House is along the lane off main road through village. But entry to grounds and studios is only by appointment and only during the summer months.

Many of the most impressive works of the late Henry Moore, OM, CH, are best seen in the open air, against the background of nature which he drew upon for inspiration. Among his larger works to be seen in the spacious grounds around the Henry Moore Foundation at Dane Tree House, Perry Green, is the one pictured here, Three-piece Sculpture: Vertebrae 1968-69, a bronze about 25 feet long and eight feet high.

The Henry Moore Foundation, a charity created by Moore in 1977, sponsors many art projects and gives grants to young sculptors each year.

Visitors to Perry Green may well be shown round by one of the

Henry Moore's 'Three-Piece Sculpture:
Vertebrae' at Perry Green

several assistants who actually worked with Moore, and one is guaranteed an informed commentary on the sculptor's life and impressions of what he was like to work with and for.

A warm-hearted Yorkshireman, Henry Moore died in 1986 at the age of 88. He and his wife Irina had lived in Perry Green since being bombed out of their Hampstead house and studio in 1940. Moore became an official war artist, making a strong impression on the public with his series of studies of sleeping figures in Underground station air-raid shelters during the Blitz. In the 1950s and 1960s his innovatory work as a sculptor was derided by many traditionalists, who failed to understand what Moore was trying to achieve; but he grew in stature, like one of his monumental bronzes, until he came to be regarded as the greatest sculptor of the 20th century.

At Perry Green, in the studios scattered about the grounds, one can study a multitude of artefacts in their various stages, which demonstrate how the master went to work. A maquette, or model, only a few inches high, would be translated into a larger model, then scaled up with the aid of assistants into a massive bronze, full of the familiar knobs, curves and holes and spindly limbs.

Moore always delighted in seeing children scrambling over his sculptures, peering through the holes and squeezing between the various figures and shapes. But humanity was, after all, the raw material of much of his work.

Places of Interest in the Neighbourhood
An Empire Builder's House (Bishop's Stortford)
A Picture in Brass (Hunsdon)
Dick Whittington, Lord of the Manor (Thorley)

54 A War Leader's Last Resting-place

Position: Ridge, near South Mimms.
O.S. Map: Luton & Hertford area: Sheet 166; 1/50,000.
Map Ref: TL 214/005.
Access: Exit Junction 23 on M25 to B157, then left into Greyhound
Lane and follow signs to Ridge along Crossoaks Lane. Church is
opposite the Old Guinea public house; grave is a few yards through
churchyard gate in Deves Hall Lane, which runs alongside church.

Beneath a plain white stone slab in this peaceful churchyard is buried
one of the great military leaders of World War II: Field Marshal the lst
Earl Alexander of Tunis (1891-1969). Visitors may wonder why he lies
here and not, perhaps, in some nobler setting such as Westminster
Abbey or St Paul's Cathedral. But his family lived at Tyttenhanger, a
17th-century house not far away (not open to the public), and he was
buried in Ridge at his own request.

It was said of Alexander that throughout his career he had that
supreme attribute as a leader, the capacity, in Kipling's phrase in 'If',
'to meet triumph and disaster and treat those two impostors just the
same.'

He fought with distinction in World War I, but it was his leadership
in World War II that won him public admiration. He commanded the
lst Corps in France in 1939, and then the ill-fated British Expeditionary
Force, refusing to leave the Dunkirk beaches until all were aboard the
rescue ships. At that time a major-general, he cruised along the shore in
a motor-boat, shouting through a loud-hailer in English and French for
possible stragglers. Only then did he save himself.

Alexander's greatest achievements were in Burma against the
Japanese, and in North Africa against the Germans. After the war he
became Governor-General of Canada and was British Minister of
Defence in the 1950s.

Alexander may have been a less flamboyant figure than some other
war leaders, but he was courageous, wise and always calm in his
judgments. He had a gift for inspiring confidence, and was particularly
adept at commanding forces of mixed nationalities.

The public held the Field Marshal in high regard, referring to him
always as 'Alex'. And it is 'In Memory of Alex' that is inscribed on his
gravestone. His wife Margaret (1905-1977) is buried with him.

Places of Interest in the Neighbourhood
  Home of Miss Muffet? (Brookmans Park)
  'Customs' Posts for Coal (Brookmans Park)

55 The Enigma of the Cave

Position: Royston, north Herts.
O.S. Map: Chelmsford & Harlow area; Sheet 167; 1/50,000.
Map Ref: TL 357/407.
Access: From north side of Melbourn Street, a few yards east of junction with Kneesworth Street; through archway to door immediately on right to Royston Cave.

Beneath one of Royston's busy streets lies one of the county's enigmas: a huge bell-shaped chamber cut in solid chalk 30ft deep and 20ft in diameter at its base – a structure unique in Britain.

Royston cave has puzzled antiquaries ever since it was accidentally discovered by market workmen in 1742. They were improving the shelter used by the market women, and while digging, struck a millstone, beneath which was the cave. However, they appeared uninterested in the carvings they found. The passage now leading visitors down to the cave was dug out in 1790 – by a local contractor who wanted to connect his premises with the cave.

What can be seen now is an impressive display of carvings all around the circular wall – the highest of them not much above head height. Many of the figures portrayed are saints and are recognisable: Christ appears in a crucifixion group, which probably includes Mary and John; and there are Richard I and his queen; and St Katherine, holding a wheel symbolising the spiked one on which she was martyred. St Laurence, who was martyred by being roasted alive on a red-hot grid, is observed holding the grid-iron; and St Christopher is seen carrying his staff with the boy Jesus.

Why the cave is there no-one knows. Some experts believe that at one time it was used as a hermitage, because there are traces of an upper floor. Some believe that it dates to the time of the Druids; others associate it with the medieval Knights Templar.

Although the cave belongs to Royston Council, it is manned by members of the local history society, and is open to the public on Saturdays, Sundays and Bank Holidays.

Places of Interest in the Neighbourhood
    Lament of the Black Death (Ashwell)
    A Gift of Milestones (Barkway)
    A Sign of the Chase (Barley)

Verulamium Roman theatre

56 Playhouse of the Legions

Position: On the west side of St Albans.
O.S. Map: Luton & Hertford area; Sheet 166; 1/50,000.
Map Ref: TL 134/074.
Access: For Verulamium theatre, leave St Albans city centre by
Fishpool St and St Michael's St, cross A414 into short lane.

The fine theatre of Roman Verulamium is almost unique – there is only
one other in Britain, at Caerleon in Wales. The theatre ruins here make
it perfectly possible to visualise the complete building, with tiered
seating – now seen as turfed banks – reconstructed stone column,
stage, dressing rooms, arena and gangways.

The theatre stands on land forming part of the Gorhambury estate,
once the home of the Bacon family and the Earls of Verulam. The
theatre was discovered in 1847, then filled in again, but in the 1930s, the
then Earl financed its re-excavation and opened it to the public.

Near the theatre are marked out ground plans of a 2nd-century town
house, and of a number of shops which fell victim to the fire-raising
tactics of Boudicca, queen of the Iceni, in her war of attrition against
the Roman invaders in 60 AD.

In 1953, in a Roman bronze-worker's shop here, was found a
delightful statuette of the Roman goddess Venus, only 21cm high: it had
lain in a box of scrap metal ready for melting down, possibly into
coinage. The statuette was rescued and is now a special exhibit, among
hundreds of other impressive artefacts, in the nearby Verulamium
Museum, a few hundred yards to the east.

Places of Interest in the Neighbourhood
    Roses, Roses All the Way (Chiswell Green)
    The Violin that Plays Itself (St Albans)
    The Inn that was Once a Cockpit (St Albans)

57 The Inn that was Once a Cockpit

Position: St Albans.
O.S. Map: Luton & Hertford area; Sheet 166; 1/50,000.
Map Ref: TL 142/069.
Access: Ye Olde Fighting Cocks is across the green south-west from St Albans Cathedral, or down Abbey Hill Lane.

The inn called Ye Olde Fighting Cocks, situated below St Albans Cathedral alongside the peaceful little river Ver, has had a varied history. As a sign explains, the Old Round House was rebuilt after the flood of 1599.

The octagonal bar was originally a medieval pigeon house c. 1400. Part of the monastery founded by King Offa of Mercia c. 798, it became the local centre for cockfighting in the 17th and 18th centuries but was renamed The Fisherman when the sport became illegal in 1849.

The Fighting Cocks appears in 'The Guinness Book of Records' as 'a foremost claimant to being the United Kingdom's oldest inn'.

Places of Interest in the Neighbourhood
Roses, Roses All the Way (Chiswell Green)
Playhouse of the Legions (St Albans)
That Wicked Lady (Wheathampstead)

90

58 The Violin that Plays Itself

Position: St Albans.
O.S. Map: Luton & Hertford area; Sheet 166; 1/50,000.
Map Ref: TL 167/066.
Position: The Organ Museum is on the east side of St Albans, at No.
320 Camp Road, next to Camp School.

The self-playing violin, with piano accompaniment, is one of the most
fascinating of the many mechanical musical instruments in this rarity
among museums. It is a Violano Virtuoso, patented in 1912 and made
in Chicago – an example of instruments once to be found in gambling
establishments and arcades in America. Violin and 44-note piano are
played electrically, by means of a perforated paper roll, similar to a
player piano roll but larger. The punched holes are 'read' by 123
electrical contacts.

The museum, based on the private collection of Mr Charles Hart,
who died in 1983, is being carried on by the St Albans Musical Museum
Society. Its atmosphere is reminiscent of an olde-worlde fairground –
with four huge illuminated pipe organs and much delightful art deco
wood carving – three disc-operated Victorian musical boxes, including
one of the kind that would be a feature in public houses, and two
theatre organs, including a mighty Wurlitzer, which once graced North
London cinemas.

On Sunday afternoons, the society's members entertain visitors (it is
open to the public) with extracts from the instruments' repertoires –
two hours of music with its own individual charm. Accordions play, so
do saxophones, drums and cymbals – all motivated by the invisible
hands of paper rolls, air and electricity.

Places of Interest in the Neighbourhood
  Roses, Roses All the Way (Chiswell Green)
  Playhouse of the Legions (St Albans)
  That Wicked Lady (Wheathampstead)

59 Church of the Horse

Position: St Ippollitts, south-east of Hitchin.
O.S. Map: Luton & Hertford area; Sheet 166; 1/50,000.
Map Ref: TL 198/271.
Access: The turning off London Road north of St Ibbs Farm leads to St Ippollitts village; the church is on the right.

Why is the figure of a horse given such prominence in this fine medieval church of St Ippolyts? There is a prancing horse on the lectern, and another on the church banner.

The reason is that the church is dedicated (uniquely in Hertfordshire) to St Hippolytus, a Roman theologian who was martyred in 236 AD and who also became the patron saint of horses, his association with them probably deriving from Greek legend – the Greek word 'hippo' meaning horse.

Among those who are supposed to have taken their horses to the church were the Knights of Temple Dinsley, Preston, a village about two miles away. Before the knights left for the crusades they would ride to St Ippolyts for a blessing. The crosses on the church's pillars are said to have been cut with their swords when they left.

Places of Interest in the Neighbourhood
  The Tragedy of Two Air Pioneers (Hitchin)
  Sir Ebenezer's Dream (Letchworth)
  The Hermit of Redcoats (Titmore Green)

The lectern, carved with a horse, in St Ippolyt's church

60 A Right Royal Error

Position: St Paul's Walden, south of Hitchin.
O.S. Map: Luton & Hertford area; Sheet 166; 1/50,000.
Map Ref: TL 192/223.
Access: St Paul's Walden church is in village, west of B651.

The tablet in All Saints Church, St Paul's Walden,
perpetuates an interesting fallacy – that the Queen Mother was born in
this parish. It is a pardonable error, which centres on the fine
18th-century mansion of St Paul's Walden Bury about a mile to the
south-west, still owned and occupied by the Bowes Lyon family after
about 250 years. Here the Queen Mother spent much of her childhood.

Even the Queen Mother's birth certificate, which correctly records
her birth on August 4th, 1900, is incorrect in naming St Paul's Walden
Bury as her place of birth. In fact, she was born at No 20 St James's
Square, London.

Why the discrepancy? In his book, *Queen Elizabeth the Queen
Mother*, Trevor Hall mentions an oversight by the Queen Mother's
father, Lord Glamis (later the Earl of Strathmore), who in the
excitement of her birth, overran the six weeks' period of grace for
registration and was fined 7s. 6d (37p).

He then 'innocuously falsified' the place of birth, preferring that his
new daughter should have been born in this beautiful old house than in

The Queen Mother tablet at St Paul's Walden

a London town house – a mischievous piece of wishful thinking on her father's part. However, the Queen Mother, who was the ninth of 10 children in her family, was certainly baptised in St Paul's Walden church.

St Paul's Walden Bury (map ref: TL 186/216) was built in 1740, with later additions by Robert Adam in 1767. The Queen Mother spent much of her childhood enjoying the idyllic surroundings of this garden: and the public can taste something of this pleasure, as they are open on certain days in spring and summer.

The first owner of the house was Edward Gilbert, who died in 1762 and whose only grandchild Mary Eleanor Bowes, married John Lyon, the 9th Earl of Strathmore; thus did the name of Bowes Lyon originate.

Places of Interest in the Neighbourhood
Bernard Shaw's 'Dell and Dwelling' (Ayot St Lawrence)
Sir Edward's Stately Fantasy (Knebworth)
Dick Turpin's Getaway (Stevenage)

St Paul's Walden Bury, the Queen Mother's childhood home

61   The Plague Door

Position: Sarratt, north of Chorley Wood.
O.S. Map: Luton & Hertford area; Sheet 166; 1/50,000.
Map Ref: TQ 040/984.
Access: The Cock inn is in Church Lane, almost opposite the church.

There is a sinister reason why a doorway in the Cock public house is much wider than it need be: 3ft 3in. Three hundred years ago the inn was a village mortuary, and the present back door was then the front door, used for bringing in coffins, around the time of the Great Plague.

The bodies of plague victims were buried in an adjoining field. Mr Les Davies, mine host at the Cock, has tried to keep his horses there. 'But they won't stay,' he says. 'They just jump out.'

The plague of 1665 – bubonic plague, carried by rat fleas – was a resurgence of the 14th-century Black Death, which had never disappeared from England. It killed at least 75,000 of the 460,000 population of London, and quickly spread throughout the countryside. It originated in London's slums, but no-one at that time understood its cause. There had been outbreaks of plague in 1603 and 1625, but the last and worst was in 1665, the year before the Great Fire of London.

The devout tended to attribute the plague to the vengeance of God for the dissolute life of King Charles II. Nervous of the Plague, the Government withdrew to Oxford. But Samuel Pepys, the diarist, revelled in the freedom that the Plague brought him: he evacuated his wife, while he remained in London. 'I have never lived so merrily as I have done this plague time,' he noted on December 31, 1665.

By 1667 the plague had disappeared from England.

Places of Interest in the Neighbourhood
    Birthplace of England's Only Pope (Abbots Langley)
    Roses, Roses All the Way (Chiswell Green)
    Buried in the 'Wrong' Tomb? (Kings Langley)

62 Overnight Stop for Wrongdoers

Position: Shenley, near Boreham Wood.
O.S. Map: Luton & Hertford area; Sheet 166; 1/50,000.
Map Ref: TL 188/008.
Access: Take B5378 north from Boreham Wood to Shenley main street.
The 'cage' stands between the Queen Adelaide inn and the small village
pond.

Lock-ups, or cages, for local wrongdoers are unusual, though not a
rarity – there are several in Hertfordshire villages. But Shenley's is
unusual in being more than just a hut. It is circular, made of
concrete-covered brick, and domed, rather like a large version of a
bottle bank, and with a heavy wooden door.

Drunks or other minor offenders would have cooled their heels here
overnight in the 18th and 19th centuries. Above the windows are two
injunctions: 'Do well and fear not' and 'Be sober, be vigilant'.

Places of Interest in the Neighbourhood
  A Tower of 'Pudding' (Aldenham)
  The 'Wooden Wonder' (London Colney)
  A War Leader's Last Resting-place (Ridge)

Shenley cage, where wrongdoers cooled their heels

63 The Church with a Detached Tower

Position: Standon, near Puckeridge.
O.S. Map: Luton & Hertford area; Sheet 166; 1/50,000.
Map Ref: TL 396/223.
Access: St Mary's Church is beside road through village.

The design of Standon Church (St Mary's) is unique in Hertfordshire on two counts: it has an especially large west porch, and it has a detached tower, which stands beside the main building. Originally it was quite separate, until an organ loft, to house a new organ, was built in 1865.

The church is built on a slope, the east end being higher than the west, so one has to climb up steps from the nave to the chancel, reached through a beautifully carved early 13th-century chancel arch.

On the village green nearby is a huge boulder of Hertfordshire puddingstone. Pieces of it can be seen in many parts of the county, sometimes in the walls of churches. (See 'A Tower of Pudding').

Places of Interest in the Neighbourhood
  An Empire Builder's House (Bishop's Stortford)
  Man and Nature in Bronze (Perry Green)
  Dick Whittington, Lord of the Manor (Thorley)

The tower that stands beside the church at Standon

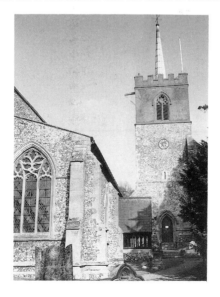

64　The First Balloon Over England

Position: Standon Green End, north of Ware.
O.S. Map: Luton & Hertford area; Sheet 166; 1/50,000.
Map Ref: TL 365/198.
Access: From A10(T), about three miles north of Ware. Turn left at
sign to Standon Green End; take footpath on left, signed to to High
Cross, and after about 100 yards turn left through wooden gate into
sheep field (close gate). The inscribed stone is railed off in the centre.

This stone marks an important aeronautical event: on September 15th,
1784, the Italian aeronaut Vincenzo Lunardi made history by making
the first balloon flight of all time over England – a daring feat only a
year after the Montgolfier brothers' first-ever balloon flight in the world
– over France.

Lunardi's ascent was from the Artillery Ground at Finsbury Square.
He touched down first at Welham Green, near Brookmans Park, in
Hertfordshire, at what is now the junction of Huggins Lane, Parsonage
Lane and Dellsome Lane (Map Ref: TL 229/056). A stone at this spot
(called locally 'Balloon Corner') announces that, 'having handed out a
cat and dog, the partners of his flight from London, he re-ascended and
continued north-eastwards'.

...But not before getting a hostile reception from the local peasantry,
who either ran away, flung themselves to the ground in fear or just
stood petrified. In fact, he handed out only his cat, which was half-dead
with cold; his dog took off again with him and he landed finally 12 miles
away in a meadow in the hamlet of Standon Green End, to much abuse
and puzzlement of the locals. A stone marks the spot, and lifting an iron

Vincenzo Lunardi

The stone marking Lunardi's touchdown after
the first balloon flight over England

flap on top reveals a pompous inscription, beginning, 'Let Posterity Know and Knowing be Astonished... The First Aerial Traveller in Britain, Mounting From the Artillery Ground in London And Traversing the Regions of the Air for Two Hours and Fifteen Minutes In this Spot Revisited the Earth'.

Lunardi's exploit won him an audience with George III and a watch from the Prince of Wales. He became an object of adulation in London society - particularly among women, who made a fashion of wearing a medallion with his portrait engraved on it.

Places of Interest in the Neighbourhood
Meeting Place of Kings (Benington)
The Church with a Detached Tower (Standon)
Anti-Slavery Memorial (Wadesmill)

65 Plotters Against Charles II

Position: Between Hoddesdon and Stanstead Abbotts.
O.S. Map: Luton & Hertford area; Sheet 166; 1/50,000.
Map Ref: TL 387/099.
Access: Rye House gate stands in a pleasant park about 200 yards north of Rye House station (BR).

This handsome gateway, a fine example of 15th-century brickwork, was once part of a house that saw the hatching of a notorious plot – the Rye House Plot – to assassinate Charles II and his brother the Duke of York (James II to be) on his way to London from Newmarket races in 1683.

One of the plotters was the tenant of Rye House, Richard Rumbold, who was a former supporter of Cromwell and an opponent of the Restoration, and is supposed to have been a guard at the execution of Charles I. The other plotters included Charles's illegitimate son, the

Duke of Monmouth, who was exiled for his part in the plot and was eventually beheaded for trying to seize the throne of James II in 1685.

The conspirators knew that the King's route from Newmarket would be along a road that narrowed as it neared Rye House. The plan was to overturn a farm cart in the path of his carriage, and to fire shots at him from the high banks on either side. But the plot went wrong because of a fire at Newmarket racecourse, bringing the king back home a week early. The plotters – about 40 in all – were betrayed and executed, imprisoned or exiled.

Although the house stands in isolation now, you can see the brick outline of the ground plan, showing the great parlour, parlour, hall, spiral staircase, kitchen and courtyard. A major restoration of the gatehouse has brought with it a fascinating exhibition telling the story behind the plot. Visitors can look through peepholes into the conspirators' room, and see and hear them discussing their plan.

The house was built in around 1443 as a fortified manor. Long after the notorious plot it became a workhouse, and in 1834 was closed down. Some years later it became a Victorian 'fun palace', complete with a maze, sports ground, boats, fairground and 'palais de danse'. The Great Bed of Ware, now in the Victoria & Albert Museum (see 'The Big Sleep'), was exhibited here between 1870 and 1927. In 1936 the house was badly damaged by fire, and until its restoration in the 1980s stood for years as a neglected ruin.

The gatehouse was bought by the Lee Valley Park in 1970. Information: tel 0992 713838.

Places of Interest in the Neighbourhood
  'Father' of the New River (Great Amwell)
  The Samaritan Woman (Hoddesdon)
  Memorial to a Park-keeper (Hunsdon)

66 Dick Turpin's Getaway

Position: Stevenage Old Town.
O.S. Map: Luton & Hertford; Sheet 166; 1/50,000.
Map Ref: TL 246/221.
Access: The Roebuck Inn is in London Road, south Stevenage.

In the late 1730s, while on the run, Dick Turpin made his last appearance in southern England. The late W. Branch Johnson, a noted Hertfordshire historian, believes this could have been at the Roebuck Hotel, Stevenage (though the present owners of the hotel, Trust House Forte, cautiously make no such claim).

Turpin, who was born in Hempstead, Essex, far from being the rather romantic figure projected in popular mythology, was in reality a ruthless rogue: there was a price on his head for murder and deer-stealing in Epping Forest. Mr Johnson's researches disclose that he intended to hide out at the Roebuck until he thought it safe to reach the alehouse at Hertford where he had arranged to meet his wife Elizabeth.

The meeting, however, never took place. Turpin is said to have spotted a constable, and escaped from the Roebuck. Later, he fled to East Yorkshire (but not on Black Bess – he never did make that legendary ride), where he was soon involved in further trouble.

The authorities, unaware of Turpin's real identity behind his alias 'Palmer', committed him to York Castle on suspicion of horse-stealing.

From behind bars in York, Turpin wrote for help to his brother-in-law in his home village, Hempstead, in Essex. Now in those days it was the recipient of a letter, not the sender, who paid the postage. Turpin's brother-in-law refused to accept the letter, which was returned to Hempstead post office. But the writing on the letter was recognised by James Smith, his old schoolmaster who, aware of his old pupil's wicked ways, travelled to York and identified 'Palmer' as Turpin.

So Turpin, who had terrorised north and east London for years as murderer and highwayman, was tried and condemned to death for the lesser (but nevertheless capital) charge of horse-stealing. He met his end on the gallows in York on March 22, 1739. And the beginning of that end was here, reportedly, at the Roebuck.

Places of Interest in the Neighbourhood
  Meeting Place of Kings (Benington)
  The Tragedy of Two Air Pioneers (Hitchin)

67 Buried at the Stake

Position: Tewin, near Hertford.
O.S. Map: Luton & Hertford area; Sheet 166; 1/50,000.
Map Ref: TL 278/168.
Access: Clibborn's post stands on the bank on the south-west side of the road between Bull's Green and Bramfield, 300 yards north of the Tewin Hill turn-off.

Beneath this strange wooden post, about five feet high, is reputed to lie the body of Walter Clibborn, who 200 years ago combined the trade of pieman with the less savoury one of leader of a robber gang. The favourite trick of the gang, which had dodged capture for months, was to earmark traders at Hertford market, dress themselves in farm labourers' smocks and lie in wait for them on the way home. A farmer at nearby Bramfield was murdered during one attack.

On December 28th, 1782, Clibborn and two accomplices ambushed a Datchworth farmer's son driving home from market, who in turn reported the attack to his uncle, Benjamin Whittenbury, at Queen Hoo Hall nearby.

Taking a servant – and a gun – the uncle and young Whittenbury set out to seek out the bandits, but this time all three were attacked. During the fight that followed Clibborn was killed. One of his companions was caught and hanged, and the other escaped. Clibborn's body was taken to the Horns public house at Bull's Green, and a coroner later adjudged the killing as justifiable homicide. Denied Christian burial, Clibborn was buried by the roadside – a fate allowed by law – with a stake driven through his body.

The original post has long since vanished, and there have been several since. The inscription on the present one, with its misspelling of Clibborn's name, bears the date 1927.

Places of Interest in the Neighbourhood
  Bernard Shaw's 'Dell and Dwelling' (Ayot St Lawrence)
  Kings of the Castle (Hertford)
  Roman Bath Under the A1 (Welwyn)

68 Dick Whittington, Lord of the Manor

Position: Thorley, south-west of Bishop's Stortford.
O.S. Map: Chelmsford & Harlow area; Sheet 167; 1/50,000.
Map Ref: TL 477/189.
Access: Thorley Hall is a private farm, but easily visible from road.

No less a personage than Dick Whittington – Sir Richard Whittington, three times Lord Mayor of London – was Lord of the Manor of Thorley, near Bishop's Stortford, in the Middle Ages.

The son of Sir William Whittington, of Pauntley, in Gloucestershire, he was Lord of the Manor from 1399 to 1413, and although there is no evidence that he lived in Thorley, he is presumed to have visited it . He served as a City of London alderman, sheriff, then as Lord Mayor of London in 1397-98, 1406-07 and 1419-20, and was a Member of Parliament in 1416.

The Whittington legend which, curiously enough, was never heard before about 1605, claims that Whittington came to London as a poor 13-year-old boy with his cat because he thought the streets were paved with gold. When he found they were not, he set out to return home, but on hearing Bow Bells as he sat on Highgate Hill, went back to London – and success.

The Whittington connection is perpetuated in Thorley: a road and a school are named after him. Several Whittington descendants have lived locally, including Alice Maria Whittington, known as 'Miss Dick', who died in 1932, having spent 40 of her 80 years in Sawbridgeworth and Bishop's Stortford. In 1930, two years before she died, 'Miss Dick' attended the Lord Mayor's Show and Banquet; thus, for her, history turned full circle.

In Thorley, Sir Richard Whittington is pre-dated by the 12th-century font and south doorway of the parish church of St James, and the chancel and nave, which are early 13th century, but not by another old building, Thorley Hall (map ref: TL 477/189) a little way east of the church, which dates from around 1435 – about 12 years after Whittington's death.

Places of Interest in the Neighbourhood
   An Empire Builder's House (Bishop's Stortford)
   Memorial to a Park-keeper (Hunsdon)
   Man and Nature in Bronze (Perry Green)

69   The Hermit of Redcoats

Position: Titmore Green, south-east of Hitchin.
O.S. Map: Luton & Hertford area; Sheet 166; 1/50,000.
Map Ref: TL 213/266.
Access: The Hermit of Redcoats inn stands on the north side of the Stevenage Road.

The sign on this inn, 'The Hermit of Redcoats', is the only visible local reminder of a famous hermit who once lived here – James Lucas (1813-1874), one of the great eccentrics of Victorian England.

When he inherited the family estate, Elmwood House (long since demolished), at Redcoats Green, Lucas refused to administer his parents' wills, deferred burial of his mother for three months, locked himself in his house and lived in the kitchen in a state of neglect and extreme squalor. He didn't wash, slept on cinders, and dressed only in a loose blanket. He protected his food – mostly bread, cheese, eggs, red herrings and gin – from rats by hanging them in a basket from the roof.

Lucas received visitors – mostly tramps - at a heavy iron grille, in the hut opposite where lived his two armed watchmen. He had distinguished visitors too, including Lord Lytton and Charles Dickens.

Dickens did not take to Lucas. He tried to write Lucas's biography, but the hermit refused. Asked if he knew of a certain pump in a certain London square, Dickens replied yes, but it was very hard to get water from. 'Well, you'll find it equally hard to pump me,' said Lucas. Dickens's own response was to portray the hermit as Mr Mopes, an unpleasant character in 'Tom Tiddler's Ground'.

The hermit was no fool. He had been well educated and had studied medicine, had a great fund of information and was a good conversationalist. Although suspicious of all his relatives (except his mother) he was kind to local children and gave them pennies, sweets and gin. In April 1874 he was found in an apoplectic fit. He died a few days later and now lies with the rest of his family in Hackney churchyard.

When the 'hermitage' was cleared, 25 years' accumulated dirt and 17 cartloads of rubbish and ashes were removed.

Places of Interest in the Neighbourhood
   The Tragedy of Two Air Pioneers (Hitchin)
   Church of the Horse (St Ippollitts)
   George Orwell's Shop (Wallington)

70 The Silent Zoo

Position: Tring, west Hertfordshire.
O.S. Map: Aylesbury & Leighton Buzzard area; Sheet 165; 1/50,000.
Map Ref: SP 923/111.
Access: The Zoological Museum is at junction of Akeman St and
Park St.

Where in Hertfordshire can you see extinct animals? Answer: the
Zoological Museum in Tring, where the quagga – a kind of South
African zebra, which died out in 1860 – is on show, as are many other
extinct and endangered species. There are also reconstructions of
dodos, a cast of an extinct giant ground sloth, and a mammoth's tusk.

One of the great advantages of 'stuffed' skins, mounted, as they are at
Tring, is that one can get a real appreciation of the size of wild creatures
– close to, and in safety! This museum, which attracts 80,000 visitors a
year and deserves to be better-known, is the place to see them.

This large collection of mammals, birds, insects and reptiles –
including an elephant, rhinos, lions and a tiger – once belonged to
Lionel Walter, the 2nd Baron Rothschild, who had a lifelong
enthusiasm for animals: he even began collecting insects at the age of
seven. In adulthood he drove a team of zebras drawing a coach along
Piccadilly.

As a young man Rothschild went into his father's bank, but his
thoughts were really elsewhere – at Tring. Whenever he could, he
would spend the evening in the laboratory at the museum. His niece
Miriam said he had only one talent with money – spending it. Which he
did, with breathtaking lavishness.

Lord Rothschild opened his museum to the public in 1892, and in
1937, when he died, he bequeathed it to the British Museum on one
condition: that, along with his library of 30,000 books, it should
become an annexe of the Natural History Museum – which it is today.

Places of Interest in the Neighbourhood
  Where the Saxons Surrendered (Berkhamsted)
  Buried in the 'Wrong' Tomb? (Kings Langley)
  The Canal Duke (Little Gaddesden)

A rhinoceros in Tring Zoological Museum

71 Anti-Slavery Memorial

Position: About 250 yards north of Wadesmill, up the A10.
O.S. Map: Luton & Hertford area; Sheet 166; 1/50,000.
Map Ref: TL 360/180.
Access: Clarkson's obelisk is on west side of Highcross Hill, next to a seat.

It was on the site of this obelisk, along what was the Cambridge Road, better known now as the A10, that the story of one of history's most impressive crusades was born. In 1785 25-year-old Thomas Clarkson decided to devote his life to the abolition of the slave trade. Thirty-three years after his death in 1846, this 7ft obelisk was erected to mark the spot where he made his decision.

Clarkson's interest in slavery was first roused when he was studying at St John's College, Cambridge, winning a prize for a Latin essay on the theme, 'Is it right to make slaves of others against their will?'. It was translated into English in 1786 and widely read.

Clarkson became obsessed by the scale and moral implications of the slavery question. Riding back to London from Cambridge one day, he dismounted and sat down at the roadside at Wadesmill. 'Here a thought came into my mind – that if the contents of the essay were true, it was time some person should see these calamities to their end. Agitated in this manner, I reached home.'

Clarkson's is a remarkable story of how personal drive can be translated into decisive political action. In 1823, during his crusade, he became a leading member of the Anti-Slavery Society. Ten years later, thanks largely to the combined efforts of Clarkson, and (in Parliament) William Wilberforce (also educated at St John's, Cambridge), slavery was abolished throughout the British Empire.

Wordsworth was so impressed with Clarkson's achievement that he wrote this fulsome sonnet to him on the occasion of the passing of the crucial Parliamentary Bill:

> Clarkson! it was an obstinate Hill to climb;
> How toilsome, nay how dire it was, by Thee
> Is known, – by none perhaps, so feelingly;
> But Thou, who, starting in thy fervent prime,
> Didst first lead forth this pilgrimage sublime,
> Hast heard the constant Voice its charge repeat,
> Which, out of thy young heart's oracular seat,
> First roused thee. – O true yoke-fellow of Time

With unabating effort, see, the palm
Is won, and by all Nations shall be worn!
The bloody Writing is for ever torn,
And Thou henceforth shalt have a good Man's calm,
A great Man's happiness; thy zeal shall find
Repose at length, firm Friend of human kind!

Places of Interest in the Neighbourhood
    The Church with a Detached Tower (Standon)
    The First Balloon Over England (Standon Green End)
    A Poet's 'Fairy Palace' (Ware)

72 The Witch Who Never Was

Position: Walkern, north-east of Stevenage.
O.S. Map: Luton & Hertford area; Sheet 166; 1/50,000.
Map Ref: TL 289/265.
Access: Manor Farm can be seen from the west side of the village High Street (B1037).

Of obvious interest is the delightful octagonal brick dovecote here which dates back to the late 17th century; it is privately owned and in fact lived in. Much less tangible in Walkern, though, was the cause célèbre involving Jane Wenham, the 'witch' who got away – the last woman in Britain to be condemned to death for witchcraft. But the sentence was never carried out.

In 1711 Jane was accused by a farmer of practising the black art on two serving maids and a boy. In recompense for the false accusation, she managed to obtain a shilling from the farmer, but the rector's servants were convinced she really was a witch, and accordingly she was ducked in the pond.

Jane was then committed to Hertford Assizes. Some time before the trial, she had apparently been intimidated into confessing to the alleged crime, later attributing the confession to fear. But in spite of the efforts of the kindly Judge Powel, the jury found her guilty. Reluctantly, the judge sentenced her to death. Later, she was reprieved and then pardoned by Queen Anne.

Jane was found a cottage in Hertingfordbury, near Hertford, by a kindly wellwisher, and she died in comparative comfort there in 1730, and was buried in the village churchyard in an unmarked grave.

The Wenham case caused widespread controversy, and under the Witchcraft Act of 1735 the death penalty, which had sent so many less fortunate women to the stake before her, was rescinded and imprisonment substituted.

Places of Interest in the Neighbourhood
  Meeting Place of Kings (Benington)
  The Tragedy of Two Air Pioneers (Hitchin)
  Dick Turpin's Getaway (Stevenage)

73 George Orwell's Shop

Position: Wallington, near Baldock.
O.S. Map: Luton & Hertford area; Sheet 166; 1/50,000.
Map Ref: TL 292/338.
Access: Orwell's cottage is in Kit's Lane (No 2), and stands beside the road at a minor T-junction.

George Orwell, pseudonym of the author Eric Blair, lived in this 300-year-old cottage for four years – 1936-1940 – when it was a rather run-down village store and somewhat tumbledown, compared with its beautifully restored condition today. Neatly thatched, it carries a county council plaque on the outside wall, noting the Orwell connection.

Orwell was in his twenties when he married his first wife Eileen O'Shaughnessy in Wallington village church. While living in Wallington he wrote *The Road to Wigan Pier* and *Homage to Catalonia*, supplementing his writing income by serving in the shop – not very efficiently, by all accounts. Many of his letters are headed 'The Stores, Wallington'.

For a time he went away to fight in the Spanish Civil War, but was soon invalided out. He returned to Wallington, but left again for Morocco to recuperate from illness. In 1940 he and his wife moved to a new home near Regent's Park.

Wallington left its mark on Orwell. He drew on his experience there for at least one book: *Animal Farm*, that vivid allegorical indictment of Communism, which partners his chillingly gloomy look into the future, *Nineteen Eighty-Four*. For the setting of *Animal Farm* is 'Manor Farm', in 'Willingdon', and there was, and is still, Manor Farm, in Wallington, only a few yards from Orwell's cottage.

Orwell, a prolific writer, later became a BBC war correspondent and newspaper and magazine columnist. He died from tuberculosis in 1950 at the age of only 46.

Places of Interest in the Neighbourhood
  Pepys Deciphered (Baldock)
  Sir Ebenezer's Dream (Letchworth)
  Miss Lawrence's Folly (Letchworth)

74 Last Journey of a Queen

Position: Waltham Cross, south of Hoddesdon.
O.S. Map: Luton & Hertford area; Sheet 166; 1/50,000.
Map Ref: TL 361/004.
Access: Eleanor Cross is at the junction of the High St and A121.

When Edward I's beloved queen, Eleanor of Castile, died of a fever in Harby (near Lincoln), in 1290, the king had her body carried to Westminster Abbey, where she lies today in the Confessor's chapel.

But so that she should not be forgotten, he had a cross erected at every spot where her coffin made an overnight stop en route, and this one at Waltham is one of only three survivors of the 12 erected to mark these resting-places. It was built in 1291 and has been carefully maintained and restored over the centuries.

Modern and medieval: the Eleanor Cross against the background of a new building at Waltham Cross

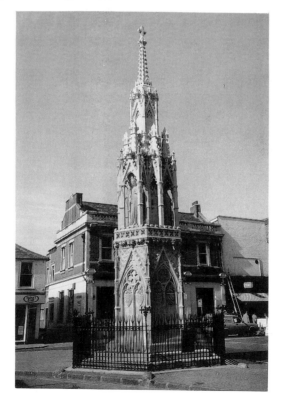

The other crosses are at Geddington (Northants) and Northampton. The one at Charing Cross, probably more famous than any, was the last on the journey to Westminster Abbey, but the existing one is in fact a Victorian copy.

The Eleanor Crosses are an important illustration of architecture's evolution in England. The cross at Waltham, for example, shows how the simplicity of Early English (the first of the four medieval gothic styles of architecture) of the bottom stage of the monument has evolved to the softer, more sophisticated flowing style of the later Decorated, higher up.

Queen Eleanor is represented by the three figures in niches under canopies.

Places of Interest in the Neighbourhood
  Wren's Banished Gateway (Cheshunt)
  The King and the Tinker (Cheshunt)

The Great Bed of Ware, now in the V & A Museum

75 The Big Sleep

Position: The Great Bed of Ware is in the Victoria & Albert Museum, Cromwell Road, London SW7

The Great Bed of Ware, though no longer in Hertfordshire and out of sight, it is certainly not out of mind. Perhaps the county should never have let it go. Today the famous relic is in the Victoria & Albert Museum, which bought it quite properly for £4,000 in 1931.

The Bed was 10ft 7ins wide, 10ft 10ins long and 8ft 9ins high. Extravagant claims were made about how many could sleep in it, and 18th-century troops were among its many occupants. One report noted that 'six citizens and their wives came from London in a frolick to sport themselves' at Ware.

The Great Bed, made in around 1590 of solid oak with marquetry panels in its headboard, had been exhibited in various parts of the county, including Rye House, at Stanstead Abbotts (see 'Plotters Against Charles II') for at least three centuries.

The Bed has been mentioned numerous times in literature. Shakespeare refers to it in *Twelfth Night* when a sheet is talked of as being 'big enough for the bed of Ware'. Dickens mentioned it in a short story, 'The Holly Tree'. It also appears in Ben Jonson's *The Alchemist*.

Victoria & Albert Museum experts refer to it as being 'middling grand': 'It probably represents the best of indigenous craftsmanship in wood of the Elizabethan period, but its fame rested from the outset on its enormous size rather than on any aesthetic merits it may have.'

But for whom was the Bed made? Take your pick of the claims: that it was ordered for the Earl of Warwick (the Kingmaker) – a clue being the carving of his bear-and-ragged-staff crest; that it was intended for the overweight King Henry VIII; that it was made by Jonas Fosbrooke, a carpenter of Ware, who gave it to Edward IV.

76 A Poet's 'Fairy Palace'

Position: Ware, near Hertford.
O.S. Map: Luton & Hertford area; Sheet 166; 1/50,000.
Map Ref: TL 357/138.
Access: Scott's grotto adjoins 28 Scott's Rd, which is alongside Ware College. Open to the public on the last Saturday afternoon of the month Apr-Sept (tel: 0920 464131). Other times by appointment.

The advice to take a torch into Scott's Grotto is certainly necessary: the place is completely in the dark. One might also be in the dark about why on earth the grotto was installed at all, except that, 200 years ago, grottoes were very much in fashion.

The grotto was built by a minor poet, John Scott, whose family had moved to Amwell House (now part of nearby Ware College) to escape smallpox. Scott re-visited London only once in 20 years, but this did not prevent visits to him by members of fashionable London society, and among Scott's weekend visitors was Dr Johnson, who said he 'loved' Scott and wanted to write his biography. He described the grotto as a 'fairy palace'.

The grotto consists of a man-made 'cave' dug 70ft into a hillside at its farthest point. It is a puzzling collection of minuscule chambers, with official-sounding names like committee rooms and refreshment, robing and consultation rooms, and the biggest, a 'council chamber'.

These are mostly only a few feet in diameter, and all are connected by a continuous, narrow, roughly circular passageway, with smaller passages leading off. There are air vents through the sides of the chambers, each of which has recessed seats. The whole construction spans about 60 feet. Scott was collecting shells and fossils in the 1760s, and his intention was to use these, along with flint decorations, for lining it.

One of his poems, the Second Elegy, seems to express Scott's yearning for a grotto, when he wrote:

> O for some secret shady cool recess,
> Some Gothic dome o'erhung with darksome trees,
> Where thick damp walls this raging heat repress,
> Where the long aisle invites the lazy breeze.

Although the project was never quite completed, there are enough wall and ceiling shell-pattern decorations – numbering thousands – to be impressive. It is said to have cost Scott around £10,000 – a prodigious sum in those days, and not an easy one to believe. 'Shady

The doorway into Scott's Grotto, Ware

and cool' the grotto certainly is, by the way, but dry, not damp.

Above the grotto is a gazebo, where John Scott is supposed to have written his famous poem 'Amwell'. This appears on the monument to Sir Hugh Myddelton, and I reproduce it in the item ' Father of the New River'.

Places of Interest in the Neighbourhood
  'Father' of the New River (Great Amwell)
  Memorial to a Park-keeper (Hunsdon)
  Plotters Against Charles II (Stanstead Abbotts)

77 Charlie Chaplin Played Here

Position: Watford.
O.S. Map: Luton & Hertford area; Sheet 166; 1/50,000.
Map Ref: TL 109/965.
Access: The Palace Theatre is in Clarendon Road, which runs from
Watford Junction station (BR) to the High Street.

During the past 80 years or so, there has been an almost constant
stream of stage stars to Watford, Hertfordshire's biggest town, there to
perform in the town's Edwardian theatre, the Palace.

Ring up the curtain at the Palace, and the ghosts of the great but gone
before flit across the stage of memory, such as Marie Lloyd, who used
to appear in the first act of the first house of the Metropolitan Edgware
Road, then pony-and-buggy it out to Watford in time for the last act in
the first house, stay to perform the first act of the second house at
Watford, then return to the Met for the last act of the evening! There
was the Fred Karno Company; there were Dan Leno jr, and Stan
Laurel. Then in the Twenties and Thirties, George Robey, Little Tich,
Bob Hope, Gracie Fields, Anton Dolin, Wendy Toye, Helen Vayne.

More recently, Sir John Mills (theatre president), Dame Wendy
Hiller, Robert Powell and Helen Mirren have appeared here, along with
Hayley Mills, Sarah Miles, Prunella Scales, Griff Rhys-Jones, Rik
Mayall, Sandra Dickinson and Sheila Steafel.

The Palace's outside aspect is very different from the time of the
opening in 1908 as the Watford Palace of Varieties. But inside, you
would hardly be surprised if Marie Lloyd were to step on stage singing
one of her famous songs: it has that unmistakable atmosphere.

The theatre opened amid much speculation as to 'what class of
entertainment can be expected'. 'It will be such,' the management
assured the public, 'as to be found in the metropolis but without the
inconvenience of an irksome railway journey.... There will be fun,
frolic, and instruction.... The programme cannot fail to be of a
high-class productive nature and free from all offence.'

In 1960, thanks to a grant of £4,500 (a useful sum then) from the
Corporation, the theatre lease passed from private into civic hands.
Hence the Watford Civic Trust Ltd, and a theatre that belongs to the
people of Watford.

Places of Interest in the Neighbourhood
  Birthplace of England's Only Pope (Abbots Langley)
  A Tower of 'Pudding' (Aldenham)
  The Poet Who Rebuked the Kaiser (Bushey)

78 Roman Bath Under the A1

Position: Welwyn bypass.
O.S. Map: Luton & Hertford area; Sheet 166; 1/50,000.
Map Ref: TL 235/160.
Access: Driving north up the A1(M), turn off at sign saying 'Welwyn A1000' (Junction 6), then follow side road straight over first roundabout. Watch out for sign saying 'Welwyn Roman Bath House' on the right of the second roundabout.

An archaeologist's chance find of Roman tiles sticking out of the bank of the river Mimram in 1960 led to an exciting find – the remains of a sprawling complex of four buildings comprising a Roman villa, or farmstead, on a site at Dicket Mead. Today, there is only one visible feature of the villa complex: a 3rd-century bathhouse, which has been preserved in a specially constructed vault directly under the A1(M). A pity that most motorists, rushing northwards and southwards are oblivious of its presence, as it has been open to the public since 1972.

The Roman bath-house under the A1 at Welwyn

Excavating the baths was a race against time for Mr Tony Rook and his fellow excavators; work had to be finished before the construction of the A1(M), in the path of which it lay. The baths are now housed in a protective steel vault beneath the motorway. A walkway all round the remains enable spectators to have an excellent view of the remains. Just to the north-east was the Lockleys Roman villa, which was excavated in 1937, but this stands on private land and now nothing of it can now be seen.

The baths themselves, which were for private use, were built around 250 AD and were in use for more than 50 years. They are equipped with cold room, warm room, hot room, cold and hot baths and furnace room. There are also the remains of a hypocaust - the Romans' form of underfloor heating using ducted warm air.

Many interesting finds were made in the Dicket Mead villa, and special environmentally controlled showcases represent items used by the people who lived there, including building materials, cooking and eating utensils, hairpins, needles, pottery, coins and jewellery.

The baths are administered by Welwyn Hatfield Museum Service.

Places of Interest in the Neighbourhood
Bernard Shaw's 'Dell and Dwelling' (Ayot St Lawrence)
Divided in Death (Ayot St Lawrence)
Buried at the Stake (Tewin)

The great railway viaduct at Digswell, near Welwyn

79 The Viaduct that Frightened Victoria

Position: South of Welwyn North station (BR).
O.S. Map: Luton & Hertford area; Sheet 166; 1:50,000.
Map Ref: TL 236/150.
Access: Digswell Viaduct passes over the B1000, north of Welwyn
Garden City.

There is a story, now firmly entrenched in local lore, concerning Queen
Victoria and the Digswell Viaduct at Welwyn. The viaduct, among the
finest in Britain and one of the county's architectural wonders, was
built in 1850 to span the Mimram valley, when the Great Northern
Railway was being laid between London and Peterborough.

On August 25th, 1851, the Queen travelled on this line to Balmoral.
But when she reached Digswell viaduct, she was overcome by
nervousness and, preferring to view it from a safe distance, stopped the
train and was conveyed across the valley by coach. Then she boarded
the train the other side, at Welwyn North station.

Less intimidated was Blondin, who is supposed to have practised his
tightrope walking across the Mimram valley before his perilous trip
across Niagara in 1859, blindfolded and pushing a wheelbarrow.

The viaduct leaps over the Mimram valley with 40 30ft-span arches,
98 feet from the river at the highest point and extending to 500 yards.
Designed by Lewis Cubitt and built by Thomas Brassey, this Grade II
listed structure took two years to complete. It has several times been
added to: there was tie-rod strengthening in 1858, eight years after it
was built; an outer skin of blue facing bricks was completed in 1935;
and tie bars were provided to reinforce the two brick skins in 1965;
drains and waterproofing were added in 1986.

Places of Interest in the Neighbourhood
   Bernard Shaw's 'Dell and Dwelling' (Ayot St Lawrence)
   Buried at the Stake (Tewin)
   Roman Bath Under the A1 (Welwyn)

80 That Wicked Lady

Position: Wheathampstead.
O.S. Map: Luton & Hertford area; Sheet 166; 1/50,000.
Map Ref: TL 170/128.
Access: Nomansland Common is at the junction of Ferrers Lane and
Green Lane.

The 17th century was not exactly noted for feminism, but the public
house here, 'The Wicked Lady', reminds us that one of the most
notorious of highwaymen was a woman – Katherine, Lady Ferrers. She
concentrated her activities around Nomansland Common, which now
serves the worthier function of a 'recreation area'. (It is called
Nomansland because it is situated on the border of lands once owned
by the abbeys of St Albans and Westminster.)

The Wicked Lady – fictionalised in two films, one starring Margaret
Lockwood and James Mason – was married at the age of 12 to the son
of Sir Simon Fanshawe, 16-year-old Thomas. Not surprisingly, the

The sign of The Wicked Lady, Coleman Green

marriage was a failure, so, neglected by her husband, she went to live alone in her father's former house, Markyate Cell, a medieval hermitage (map ref: TL 059/172) six or seven miles to the north-east of Nomansland.

While living there, Lady Ferrers met a Ralph Chaplin, a farmer by day but a highwayman by night – literally a moonlighter. It was he who initiated Katherine into his own nefarious ways, and preyed on travellers around Markyate.

Chaplin himself was shot while marauding on Finchley Common, North London, but Katherine's last highway adventure was near Nomansland. One evening, at dusk, masked as usual, she picked on a waggon as her quarry, believing that the waggoner was alone. However, he had earlier given two men a lift, and one of them, hidden among bales and armed with a gun, fired and hit her ladyship. Bleeding and weakened, she made for Markyate Cell, and just managed to reach there before she died.

The building occupied by Lady Ferrers has been replaced by a 19th-century mansion, which incorporates the remains of a previous one. Lady Katherine's ghost is said to haunt the area. It was observed by workmen in 1840, and by several people at a parish tea, and around the turn of the century, Mr Ady, the then occupant of Markyate Cell, repeatedly saw Lady Ferrers's ghost on the stairs. She has also been reported galloping through the lanes around Nomansland.

Places of Interest in the Neighbourhood
   Bernard Shaw's 'Dell and Dwelling' (Ayot St Lawrence)
   Bunyan's Chimney (Coleman Green)
   Where Old Battles Were Fought (Wheathampstead)

81 Where Old Battles Were Fought

Position: Wheathampstead.
O.S. Map: Luton & Hertford area; Sheet 166; 1/50,000.
Map Ref: TL 186/135.
Access: To reach Devil's Dyke, walk down Dyke Lane, off Marford
Road, passing through an iron gate. To reach The Slad, go up the
narrow Beech Hyde Lane for half a mile, walk eastwards along track at
edge of field.

Centuries ago, on the outskirts of what is now Wheathampstead, two
great earthworks were scooped out, their banks being built up as
military defences. They can still be seen. Devil's Dyke is nearly 500
yards long, about 40 yards wide and was at one time 40 feet deep. To
the east of it is The Slad, a marshy ditch slightly shorter and narrower
than Devil's Dyke.

The ditches are thought to have been dug to defend an ancient
encampment, the headquarters of Cassivellaunus, chief of the Belgic
Catuvellauni tribe, who stood up to the Romans under Julius Caesar on
his expedition of 54 BC. Caesar had overwhelmed the Catuvellauni
when crossing the Thames, and then marched northwards.

The celebrated archaeologist Sir Mortimer Wheeler excavated the site
in 1932 and found evidence of occupation by the Belgic tribe. In 'De
Bello Gallico' (The Gallic War), Caesar himself describes a battle
believed to have been the one fought here.

Places of Interest in the Neighbourhood
   Bernard Shaw's 'Dell and Dwelling' (Ayot St Lawrence)
   Bunyan's Chimney (Coleman Green)
   That Wicked Lady (Wheathampstead)

82 In Loving Memory...

Every county has its interesting graves. Here is a selection in Hertfordshire – a selection only, not a comprehensive list.

Vandalism is not a modern phenomenon – body-snatching was an unsavoury feature of the early 19th century, when the number of corpses available for medical dissection lagged far behind the need for them. John Gootheridge, a churchwarden and farmer, was buried twice within a week in *Codicote* churchyard (map ref: TL 218/187) in 1824; taken by body-snatchers, his body was recovered and reburied a week later. These so-called 'resurrection men' could make between £8 and £10 a time for bodies – many hundreds of pounds in today's terms.

Peter the Wild Boy, buried in *Northchurch* churchyard, near Berkhamsted (map ref: SP 974/088), had captured royal attention in his youth. He had been found at the age of 13 wandering in a forest in Germany, near Hanover, living like an animal. George I took an interest in him and put him in a home in England, but he resisted all attempts to teach or train him. So Peter was sent to a farm, where he died in 1785, aged 72.

Visitors from all over the world go to see the strange tomb of Lady Anne Grimston, buried at *Tewin*, near Hertford (map ref: TL 268/143) in 1710. She was allegedly a Sadducean – one who did not believe in the resurrection of the dead (though the church itself notes that she was a regular weekly attender at services). Lady Anne is supposed to have said: 'If, indeed, there is a life hereafter, trees will rend asunder my tomb.' Well, the tomb certainly is rent asunder – by ash trees and sycamores. But which came first, the myth or the trees?

In this churchyard are three members of a famous aeronautical family, the De Havillands. The brave pilot, Geoffrey, was killed in his 37th year in 1946, while testing an aircraft over the Thames Estuary before making an attempt on the world air speed record. (His air pioneer father, Sir Geoffrey, founded the famous De Havilland aircraft company, based at Hatfield).

Also buried here are his mother, Lady Louise, and her son John, like his brother the victim of an aircraft accident, in 1943. 'They gave their lives in advancing the science of flight,' reads the inscription. 'To strive, to seek, to find and not to yield.'

In *Ware* churchyard (map ref: TL 357/143) there is a strange grave that tells a lie. Beneath a slab level with the ground is the body of Dr William Meade, who died in 1652, aged – according to the fast-fading inscription – 148 years, 9 months, 3 weeks and 4 days. Apparently this inscription (which is not the original one) was put there as a joke by a contemporary local chemist who stocked Dr Meade's Patent Medicine.

And there is the famous Jack O'Legs, subject of an intriguing headboard in the churchyard at *Weston* (about four miles east of Hitchin, map ref: TL 266/300). He was a Robin Hood-like character, it seems: a robber giant who centuries ago lived in a nearby wood. Jack O'Legs would attack Baldock bakers who gave short weight or overcharged, then give the proceeds to the poor. But he was also a highwayman, and when the bakers caught him, they decided to kill him. But they allowed him a final wish, so he asked to die where his arrow fell. It flew three miles (that's the story) and landed in this churchyard, between two stones 12 feet apart. Which is where the headboard stands.

Hertfordshire also houses the graves of two notable seafarers. Vice-Admiral Sir Sydney Fremantle, who died in 1958 at the age of 90, is buried in *Essendon* churchyard (map ref: TL 274/088). Descended from one of Nelson's sea captains, he was the senior naval officer at Scapa Flow on June 21st, 1919, the day the Versailles Treaty came into force.

By mischance or error of judgment, he had decided to take all his ships to sea on that day, thus missing the momentous scuttling of almost the entire German fleet of 70 warships. He accused the Germans of violating 'all the decent laws and rules of the seas', but his absence at this crucial moment involved him in controversy, which he could never quite live down.

Finally, in *Little Hadham* churchyard (map ref: TL 446/228) lies Captain William Harvey, who died in 1807 at the age of 65. He sailed as a midshipman three times with Captain Cook, and was with him on his last voyage to the Sandwich Islands.

Body-snatchers passed this way... the grave
of John Gootheridge at Codicote

Index

The Curiosities of England

The following titles in the series have already been published and can be ordered at all bookshops, or in case of difficulties direct from the publishers.

Buckinghamshire Curiosities John Lucas 1 874336 11 3

Cheshire Curiosities Peter Bamford 0 946159 96 3

Cotswold Curiosities Reginald Dixon 0 946159 51 1

Dorset Curiosities George Osborn 0 946159 38 6

East Anglian Curiosities Rick O'Brien 0 946159 97 1

Hampshire Curiosities Jo Daper 0 946159 57 2

Hertfordshire Curiosities John Lucas 0 946159 75 0

Isle of Wight Curiosities Jack Jones 0 946159 67 X

Kent Curiosities John Vigar 0 946159 95 5

Northamptonshire Curiosities Chris Billing 1 874336 12 1

North and East Yorkshire Curiosities Duncan & Trevor Smith
1 874336 09 1

Nottinghamshire Curiosities Geoffrey Oldfield 0 946159 98 X

Somerset Curiosities Enid Byford 0 946159 48 3

South and West Yorkshire Curiosities Duncan & Trevor Smith
0 946159 99 8